SEPARATING SCHOOL & STATE

How to Liberate America's Families

THE FUTURE OF FREEDOM FOUNDATION

Sheldon Richman

The Future of Freedom Foundation
• Fairfax, Virginia •

ISBN 0-9640447-1-4 — ISBN 0-9640447-2-2 (pbk.)
Third printing, Copyright © 1995

The Future of Freedom Foundation
11350 Random Hills Road, Suite 800
Fairfax, Virginia 22030

Library of Congress
Catalog Card Number: 94-072163

Printed in the United States of America

Cover art by Susan Somerfield Stoffle

To Kathleen, Jennifer, Emily, and Ben, with love;

in loving memory of my father and in honor of my mother—
who believed in me when my school counselor did not;

also, in memory of John Holt, Roy A. Childs, Jr., and Karl Hess.

Contents

The fundamental theory of liberty upon which all governments in this Union repose excludes any general power of the State to standardize its children by forcing them to accept instruction from public teachers only. The child is not the mere creature of the State. . . .

—U.S. Supreme Court
Pierce v. Society of Sisters, 1925

It is only from a special point of view that "education" is a failure. As to its own purposes, it is an unqualified success. One of its purposes is to serve as a massive tax-supported jobs program for legions of not especially able or talented people. As social programs go, it's a good one. The pay isn't high, but the risk is low, the standards are lenient, entry is easy, and job security is still pretty good. . . . In fact, the system is perfect, except for one little detail. We must find a way to get the children out of it.

—Richard Mitchell
The Leaning Tower of Babel

Acknowledgments

Thanks to Jacob G. Hornberger of the Future of Freedom Foundation and Alex Chafuen of the Atlas Economic Research Foundation for their support, financial and intellectual. Jacob Hornberger deserves additional gratitude for suggesting this project and for showing heroic patience when my work was in its less tangible stages. His enthusiasm and encouragement were the tonic that every author needs. Over the years I have benefited from many discussions on political, economic, and historical issues related, however remotely, to public education. Among those from whom I have learned much are my good friends Ralph Raico, Leonard Liggio, Roy Cordato, Jeffrey Rogers Hummel, Joseph Sobran, Brian Doherty, and David Boaz. Additionally, Ralph Raico, Brian Doherty, David Boaz, and Patrick Farenga read the manuscript and made important suggestions. Of course, none of these people are responsible for any surviving errors. (The one who *is* responsible shall remain nameless.)

Two special thank-yous to people I unfortunately never met, but whose influence is reflected in this book: John Taylor Gatto's and the late John Holt's fertile writings on education and how children learn have meant more to me than I can say.

My thanks to Ron Neff and Storme O'Keefe for their careful proofreading, Shirley Kessel for her index, and Susan Somerfield Stoffle for her fine cover art.

My wife, Kathleen, is due special thanks for her understanding of my need to get this book finished. My children—Jennifer, Emily, and Ben—graciously gave up some "special time" for this cause. They have taught me everything I know about kids and much of what I know about education.

Preface

Whehn the Berlin Wall collapsed and the Soviet empire disintegrated, Americans took great pride in their heritage of individual liberty and free markets. "Capitalism is superior to socialism," Americans told the world. "Free enterprise is the economic system the world should adopt."

Yet, despite their apparent devotion to freedom, Americans refuse to let go of *their* model of socialist, central planning: public schooling, an institution that is found in Russia, China, Cuba, the United States, and all other countries of the world.

How does public schooling work? It is run by a political commission, either at the local, state, or national level, by which politicians or bureaucrats plan the educational decisions of thousands, sometimes millions, of children. How is it funded? The state uses its coercive power of taxation to take money from some, even those who do not have children, to fund the schooling of others—a perfect embodiment of the Marxian principle, "From each according to ability, to each according to need." What do the students learn? They learn official, approved doctrine from government-approved schoolteachers who use government-approved textbooks. How do public schools get their customers? Through compulsory attendance laws by which adults are commanded to deliver their children at the age of six to these government-approved institutions.

Sheldon Richman's thesis in this book is a powerful one—and one that is certain to startle people: public schooling has proven to be a tremendous success. Why? Not because it has educated people, but because it has fulfilled the primary goal of those who instituted public schooling one hundred years ago: to create a nation of good, little citizens who view the government as their daddy—a daddy that takes care of them—and disciplines them—from the cradle to the grave.

Ultimately, however, the case against public schooling rests on moral principles, rather than on results. Should the state have the power to take children from their families to put them into state-approved institutions to receive state-approved indoctrination? Should the state have the power to take money from some in order to fund the schooling of others? Should educational decisions be made by politicians and bureaucrats, rather than by parents?

The solution to the crisis in education lies not in reform, as the supporters of public schooling so often tell us. The answer lies in the separation of school and state—the repeal of all compulsory-attendance laws and school taxes—the end of all government involvement in education.

"But education is too important to be left to the free market," the supporters of public schools tell us. Actually, education, like religion, is too important to be left in the hands of the state.

What would education look like under a free market? As with religion, families would decide the best educational vehicles for each of their children. And entrepreneurs in the educational marketplace would provide those vehicles. There would be Christian schools (with daily prayer), secular schools, music schools, and sometimes schools in the parental workplace. As Mr. Richman points out, it is impossible to predict the fantastic results that will flow from educational freedom. And how would the poor get educated? The way they were educated throughout the 1800s in the U.S., before public schooling was implemented—through fellowships, scholarships, and other financial assistance provided by the wealthier members of society, on a purely voluntary basis.

It is time for the American people to rediscover and move toward the principles of individual liberty and free markets of their ancestors—and to lead the world out of the socialist darkness of the twentieth century. The best place to begin is to liberate America's families through the separation of school and state.

—*Jacob G. Hornberger*
Founder and President
The Future of Freedom Foundation

Introduction

T he continuing crisis in public education in America has reached
a critical point. After decades of argument, debate, and experimen-
tation, it has become increasingly clear that reform programs and
refinancing gimmickry will not fundamentally improve the system.
Radical change—not Band-Aid solutions—is the only procedure that
will save American education.

Why has public schooling reached this stage of deterioration
and level of disappointment in the eyes of practically everyone? The
reason is one that most Americans feel uncomfortable admitting: the
public school system has failed because it is a system of socialist
education. And, as a result, it has manifested all the symptoms and
consequences that have usually been observed in all other examples
of socialist enterprises.

Having a near-monopoly control over the supply of educational
services in the United States, those who manage and work in the
public schools have lost all attention to the needs of the consuming
public. Indeed, parents often appear to be unavoidable nuisances
who interfere in the teachers' and administrators' belief that they
know better than the consuming public the educational product
parents and children should want. Parents, it is true, can opt out of
the system, but only if they are willing and able to pay a double
tuition—one in the form of compulsory taxation for the educational
product they do not want, and the other in the form of a voluntary fee
for the private educational services they actually want their children
to have. It is that high cost of private educational alternatives that
enables the public educational establishment to be insensitive to the

wishes of parents and children; and since taxes are paid whether or not the parents and children choose to leave the public school system, there is none of the negative financial feedback that exists in a free market to inform the supplier that he had better improve the quality of his product if he is not to run the risk of going under.

Furthermore, as a state-enforced monopoly, there is no way to discover whether the amount and the types of education supplied by the public school system are the ones that people actually want. In any normal market, the varieties of any product offered reflect the tastes and preferences of the buying public, and the qualities and characteristics of the product change over time as a response to any modification in the wants and desires of the consumers purchasing the product offered for sale. But with public schooling's being a state-enforced monopoly, new suppliers of educational services cannot freely and easily enter the market to offer something closer to what parents are looking for in terms of course-curriculum and school facilities. It is not surprising, therefore, that so many parents and students view the public school experience as a frustrating failure. Without a real, private competitive market for education in America, all that is available is what the state education central planners choose to provide.

And what is it that the state educational establishment force-feeds the school-age population? While it may, again, make many Americans uncomfortable to admit it, what the public school system imposes is an official and, many times, informal political and cultural ideology. As Sheldon Richman documents with great care in this book, modern, universal compulsory education has its origin in the 19th-century Prussian idea that it is the duty and responsibility of the state to indoctrinate each new generation of children into being good, obedient subjects who will be loyal and subservient to political authority and to the legitimacy of the political order. Young minds are to be filled with a certain set of ideas that reflect the vision of the official state educators concerning "proper behavior" and "good citizenship."

Over the generations, the content of what proper behavior and good citizenship means has changed, with changes in prevailing political and cultural currents in America, but the fact remains that the essence of the system was designed with that purpose in mind, and still operates on that basis. The parent has been viewed—and still is viewed—as a backward and harmful influence in the formative years of the child's upbringing, an influence that must be corrected for and replaced by the "enlightened" professional teacher who has been trained, appointed, and funded by the state. The public school, therefore, is a "reeducation camp" in which the child is to be remade in the proper "politically correct" image.

In the 20th century, the importance of government-controlled education was understood and exploited to the greatest degree by the totalitarian states. Through the vehicles of mandatory attendance and monopoly control over curriculum, the totalitarian states saw public schools as the means to mold the population into a harmonious collective will obedient to the dictates of those possessing absolute political authority. It was not sufficient for the great dictators of our century to have their commands obeyed under the threat of force; their ultimate goal was to control the minds of the population, and, through that method, obtain voluntary obedience from the masses over whom they ruled.

By controlling the education process, the totalitarians argued, they could manipulate the knowledge possessed and the ideas believed in by the population as a whole. Shortly after the Bolshevik Revolution in Russia, in 1918, at a congress of Party education workers, it was stated:

> We must create out of the younger generation a generation of Communists. We must turn children, who can be shaped like wax, into real, good Communists. . . . We must remove the children from the crude influence of their families. We must take them over and, to speak frankly, nationalize them. From the first days of their lives they will be under the healthy influence of Communist children's nurseries and schools. There they will grow up to be real Communists.[1]

In one of the leading pedagogical textbooks used in Soviet Russia in the 1940s, the authors argued:

> Education for us is a vital public concern and is directed toward the strengthening of the socialist state. . . . We must develop in [every child] a feeling of pride in the most revolutionary class, the working class, and in its vanguard, the Communist Party. . . . We must tell [every child] how the great people of our epoch—Lenin, Stalin, and their companions in arms—organized the workers in the struggle for a new and happy life. Our youth must be trained in militant readiness for the defense of their socialist fatherland. . . . The entire work of the school must be directed toward the education of children in communist morality. In giving knowledge to pupils and in formulating their work outlook, the school must cultivate in them habits of

communist conduct. . . . Our task in the school is not merely the education of individual children, but also and especially the education of a collective and the education of each child in the spirit of collectivism. . . . Pupils must come to know that in our Soviet country the interests of the people are inseparable from the interests of their government. . . . And the natural attachment to the native country is strengthened by pride in one's socialist Motherland, in the Bolshevik Party, in the leader of the workers of the entire world—Comrade Stalin. . . . A conscious state of discipline is an organic part of communist morality, it is cultivated throughout the program of communist education. . . . Submission to the will of the leader is a necessary and essential mark of discipline. . . . If an order is given, it must be carried out absolutely.[2]

The same was true in fascist Italy under Benito Mussolini, who declared:

The foundation of Fascism is the conception of the State, its character, its duty and its aim. Fascism conceives of the State as an absolute, in comparison with which the individuals or groups are relative, only to be conceived of in relation to the State. . . . It is the State which educates its citizens in civic virtue, gives them a consciousness of their mission and welds them into unity.[3]

In 1939, the fascist education theorist Giuseppe Bottai insisted:

To all the effective possibility of enrolling in school and following a course of study, but to each one the duty of fulfilling his scholastic obligation in the interest of the State, that is, according to his truest aptitudes, committing all his faculties and his entire responsibility in such a way that the schools may be the reserve from which the State continually draws all the fresh energy it needs and not simply the agency in which thoughtless bourgeois vanity looks for seals and diplomas for its sterile ambitions.[4]

In 1937, for example, third-grade students in Italian public schools were given the following sentence for penmanship practice: "All knots were cut by our shining sword, and the African victory [the Italian conquest of Ethiopia] will remain complete and pure in the history of the Fatherland, as the fallen and surviving legionnaires dreamt of it and wished it." In the arithmetic exercises the following problem had to be solved: "*Mussolini the Teacher*. In 1902 the salary of Mussolini the teacher was 56 lire a month. How much a day? A year?" A third-grade reader contained the following lesson to live by: " 'Obey because you must obey.' —Mussolini. With our obedience we give to the *Duce* the gift of our hardened will."[5]

In 1937, after spending almost a year and a half living under and studying the new order in Nazi Germany, Australian historian Stephen H. Roberts published a book entitled, *The House That Hitler Built*. This is his description of public education under National Socialism:

> The Nazis have laid a heavy hand on education. They know that the textbooks of to-day are shaping the political realities of the decades to come, and accordingly have made every part of education—curiously enough, even mathematics—a training ground in Nazi ideology. As soon as the child enters an elementary school *(Grundschule)* at the age of six, his days are given over to the idealizing of the Nazis. He counts up storm troopers, he sews crude figures of Black Guards, he is told fairy tales of the Nazi knights, who saved the civilized maiden from the bad Russian gnomes, he makes flags and swastikas. After four years of this, he emerges to the *Volksschule* or *Mittelschule,* thinking of Hitler and his cabinet in the way we regard Christ and His disciples. . . . All world-history since the [first world] war has meaning only as bearing on the rise of Hitler; no other fact in the world counts as much as the new-found regeneration of the nation and the rise of the *Führer*.[6]

In 1935, Dr. Bernhard Rust, Nazi Minister of Education, informed all public school teachers:

> Teachers are directed to instruct their pupils in . . . the importance of race and heredity for the life and destiny of the German people, and to awaken in them a sense of their responsibility toward "the community of the nation". . . and the will consciously to cooperate in the racial purification of the German stock. Racial instruction is to begin with the youngest pupils (six years of age) in accordance with the desire of the Führer "that no boy or girl should leave school without complete knowledge of the necessity and meaning of blood purity." The

race idea leads to the rejection of democracy and other "equal-izing tendencies". . . and strengthens understanding of the "leadership idea."[7]

In the hands of the state, compulsory public education becomes a tool for political control and manipulation—a prime instrument for the thought police of the society. And precisely because every child passes through the same indoctrination process—learning the same "official history," the same "civic virtues," the same lessons of obedience and loyalty to the state—it becomes extremely difficult for the independent soul to free himself from the straightjacket of the ideology and values the political authorities wish to imprint upon the population under its jurisdiction. For the communists, it was the class struggle and obedience to the Party and Comrade Stalin; for the fascists, it was worship of the nation-state and obedience to the Duce; for the Nazis, it was race purity and obedience to the Führer. The content has varied, but the form has remained the same. Through the institution of compulsory state education, the child is to be molded like wax into the shape desired by the state and its education elite.

We should not believe that because ours is a freer, more democratic society, the same imprinting procedure has not occurred even here, in America. Every generation of school-age children has imprinted upon it a politically correct ideology concerning America's past and the sanctity of the role of the state in society. Practically every child in the public school system learns that the "robber barons" of the 19th century exploited the common working man; that unregulated capitalism needed to be harnessed by enlightened government regulation beginning in the Progressive era at the turn-of-the-century; that wild Wall Street speculation was a primary cause of the Great Depression; that only Franklin Roosevelt's New Deal saved America from catastrophe; and that American interven-tion in foreign wars has been necessary and inevitable, with the United States government required to be a global leader and an occasional world policeman.

Sometimes the historical myths and ideological premises change. Thirty years ago, children were still taught in public schools that Christopher Columbus's voyage was the culmination of the Age of Discovery, with his landing in the Americas and the opening up of new continents for settlement and civilization; now, Columbus is portrayed as the opening stage for a reign of mass murders and the extinction of the noble Indian tribes of America. Half a century ago, the industrialization of America was taught to be seen as the engine for progress and prosperity; today, millions of children in every public school in America are taught that industrialization has produced a squandering of the resources of the earth and threatens every living thing from the sea otter to the spotted owl. Thirty years ago, the "civic virtues" taught in public schools included the impropriety of premarital sex; today, those "civic virtues" have changed to include public school instruction in the proper use of prophylactics and the birth-control pill.

What is important is not merely the truth or validity of each of these facts, interpretations, or civic virtues. What is crucial is that they cumulatively represent the "court history" and "politically correct" views that rationalize and justify a particular cultural ideology and a set of government policies and powers over the society. They represent the official "Party line" of contemporary American politics and culture that is taught in every public school. They legitimize the existing order of things and the particular political agenda of those who control the monopoly system of compulsory education. Whether we like to admit it or not, its function is essentially the same as it was in Soviet Russia, Fascist Italy, and Nazi Germany.

If parents are to be restored to their proper status as the guardians and primary educators of the young—if schooling is to be made responsive to the wants and needs of parents and children—if the American mind is to be opened to real diversity and pluralism—if education is to be made into an actual creative learning process—then the educational system must be completely taken out of the hands of the state. Education must be comprehensively privatized, freed from all forms of government regulation and control. Education must no longer be allowed to be a vehicle for the ends of the state. It must be transformed into one of the means for individual development and self-improvement.

In *Separating School and State,* Sheldon Richman effectively and comprehensively analyzes the failures of public schooling in America and explains the ideas and ideology behind the case for compulsory education. But beyond a historical interpretation and a critical evaluation of the state of public education in America today, Mr. Richman offers a vision of what a fully privatized educational system might look like—and in what ways it would solve many, if not most, of the problems that parents, students, and even a sizable number of professional educators see as the fundamental shortcomings of the present system. It is not an exaggeration to say that Mr. Richman's book may very well move the entire debate over education in America to a higher and more fruitful level of discussion.

The Future of Freedom Foundation was founded five years ago to defend the principles of the free society and the institutions of a truly free market. But freedom, if it is to be fully restored and preserved in America, requires that the marketplace of ideas be open and competitive. That will not be completely possible until education is liberated from the hands of the state. The future of freedom is closely linked to the depoliticization and comprehensive privatization of education in America. And Sheldon Richman's book is a powerful case for separating education from the state.

—Richard M. Ebeling
Vice President of Academic Affairs
The Future of Freedom Foundation

Notes

[1] Quoted in Mikhail Heller, *Cogs in the Wheel: The Formation of Soviet Man* (New York: Alfred A. Knopf, 1988), p. 149.

[2] George S. Counts and Nucia P. Lodge, trans., *"I Want to be Like Stalin," From the Russian Text on Pedagogy* by B. N. Yesipov and N.K Goncharov (New York: The John Day Co., 1947), pp. 34, 43, 58, 85, 95-96, 109.

[3] Benito Mussolini, "The Political and Social Doctrine of Fascism," [1932] in Findley Mackenzie, ed., *Planned Society: Yesterday, Today and Tomorrow* (New York: Prentice Hall, Inc., 1937), pp. 810-811.

[4] Quoted in Edward R. Tannenbaum, *The Fascist Experience: Italian Society and Culture, 1922-1945* (New York: Basic Books, 1972), p. 162.

[5] Ibid., pp. 164-165.

[6] Stephen H. Roberts, *The House That Hitler Built* (New York: Harper & Brothers Publishers, 1937), pp. 254-255.

[7] Bernhard Rust, "Racial Instruction and the National Community," in George L. Mosse, *Nazi Culture: A Documentary History* (New York: Schocken Books, 1966), pp. 283-284.

1

W(h)ither Public Schools?

The aim of public education is not to spread enlightenment at all; it is simply to reduce as many individuals as possible to the same safe level, to breed a standard citizenry, to put down dissent and originality.
—H. L. Mencken

I s anyone happy with the public schools? It seems not. Those with no financial stake in the schools have translated their unhappiness into various reform proposals, such as charter schools or voucher plans. Those who do have a stake in the current system—the teachers' unions, for example—point to the schools' bad condition as a reason for the government to appropriate more money. Whichever way they lean, people generally believe that the schools are not doing what they are supposed to be doing.

This book will come at the issue from a different angle. Maybe the schools *are* doing precisely what they were designed to do or at least what they cannot help but do. Maybe we just do not like the results now that we see them. Someone said that the ends pre-exist in the means. Is it possible that with the public schools, we have gotten exactly what we asked for? To substantiate that charge it will be necessary not only to look closely at schools but also to pull back to gain some perspective. We will have to look at both the forest and the trees. In the chapters that follow, we will step back and consider what government-sponsored schools are by virtue of that sponsorship. We will revisit the founding of public schools to see what the architects had in mind. We will follow that with a description of the criticism leveled at public schooling, from the earliest to the most recent. We will also speculate on what things would be like if there were no public schools, if school and state were separate. At the same time, we will do something dangerous: entertain the possibility that the problem is not just the public school, but school per se. The Appendix will examine the schools empirically—the test scores, the strife, the other day-to-day indicators of failure.

Sacred schools

The public schools, despite their widely recognized problems, have a mystique that prevents people from imagining life without them. You would think we have always had them. People get nervous hearing any criticism of the schools that sounds fundamental. You may find fault with the schools, of course, and you may propose to tinker with them. But if you even imply that the schools are irretrievably lost or should be changed in some really drastic way, you will stimulate a reflex response and vicious counterattack.

Consider the case of Washington, D.C., where the superintendent of schools proposed contracting out the management of the city's worst schools to a private firm, Education Alternatives, Inc. That has been done in Baltimore and elsewhere. The reform is called "privatization," but that is misleading. Yes, the firm is private. However, a private monopoly has merely been substituted for a so-called public monopoly. Parents and children have no more choice than before. The schools are still financed by taxes. A government school board, subject to state and federal authorities, still runs things. There may be a small element of market pressure in the sense that the school board can choose not to renew the contract; it may pick another company or go back to running the schools itself. Such "privatization" is not a radical solution to the schools' problems.

But to some people it sounded radical. They reacted to the proposal as if the sacred public school system were under a deadly threat. The superintendent (he is black) was called racist by some people. That's a code word for being concerned that the best students are being held back by the worst. The Washington Teachers Union led the charge. Undoubtedly, they propagandized the students, one of whom referred to the superintendent as "our slave seller [who is] selling out education to the highest-bidding rich white owner." In the end, the superintendent had to shelve the plan for lack of support.

The day after the plan was withdrawn, *Washington Post* columnist Dorothy Gilliam displayed the knee-jerk reflex that so many have about the public schools, no matter how decrepit they get. "District schools clearly need drastic improvement," wrote Gilliam, "but there simply are some places where capitalism should never tread. Public education is one." She continued: "The success of U.S. education in the 20th century was due largely to the fact that it was a community enterprise, not a private-sector one. It is the American way for public schools to answer, through the democratic process, to the communities they serve. American leaders have long recognized the importance public education plays in creating a learned citizenry capable of maintaining a democracy." She quoted the Carnegie Foundation for the Advancement of Teaching: "The nation's public schools collectively remain one of America's most vital institutions, with the mission of sustaining a democratic nation as well as serving the individual."

Who are Gilliam and the Carnegie Foundation kidding—besides themselves? Where is the evidence that the public schools are serving communities and "maintaining democracy"? In whose dreams are they accountable through the democratic process? By what stretch of the imagination can anyone claim that education has been a success in the 20th century? Literacy was higher before government schools existed. Government historically has been a hindrance to education. In the antebellum South, it was a crime to teach slaves to read. Historian E. G. West writes that in early 19th-century England, the government complained that people were too literate and were using their skill to read seditious material. Thomas Malthus in 1803 worried that "the circulation of [Thomas] Paine's *Rights of Man* . . . has done great mischief among the lower and middle classes of this country."[1] Moreover, the public school system that is said to be so vital to America was modeled on the one designed for 19th-century Prussia, a paragon of authoritarianism, not freedom. It is hardly something Americans should be proud of. (More about that in Chapter 3.)

Gilliam is like Dorothy in *The Wizard of Oz,* clicking her heels together, squeezing her eyes shut, and endlessly—fervently—saying to herself, trying to make herself believe it, "The public schools can work. The public schools can work." But that will not make them work. Who suffers most? Not the rich and sophisticated, who always will find ways and wherewithal to get out. No, it is the poor and least knowledgeable about how to "game" the system who will be condemned to remain at the bottom. They will find no relief in the good intentions—if indeed that is what they are—of the administrators of and apologists for the public schools.

3

What is community?

Note also Gilliam's premise that the community and the private sector are at odds with each other. Schools, she said, are a community enterprise, not a private-sector one. There is no conflict, however. Private schools can be community enterprises. Home schoolers are routinely involved in community activities. Of those three kinds of educational efforts, the public schools—with their violence and failure—are the most estranged from the community. People have been so indoctrinated with the religion of state, thanks in part to the public schools, that they fail to understand that the community *is* the private sector. That term refers to all nongovernmental activities: profit-making enterprises, nonprofit organizations, voluntary efforts of all kinds, religious centers, homes, families, and more.

Gilliam's column contained another fallacy widely held by apologists for the public schools. "Corporations deal in producing products," she wrote; "Schools deal in developing human beings. There's a big difference." Those few words are fraught with error. Many corporations deal in services, not products. Some can even be said to deal in "developing human beings." Holiday Spa is a large corporation that develops the physical side of human beings. Berlitz is a large corporation that develops language skills in human beings. Harvard University and Stanford University are private corporations. But perhaps more important, *schools do not—and should not—develop human beings*. It has long been popular to think of education that way. That, I believe, is wrong. *Human beings develop themselves—if they develop at all.* To grow, children need assistance; specifically, they need information and good examples from the adults. But they do not need adults or institutions to develop them into human beings. This is not just semantics. The common conception of education casts children in a fundamentally passive role. They are empty vessels that only adults with special skills—teachers—can fill. As we will see, the architects of the public schools consistently saw the mission of education as the development of human beings. They spoke of children as formless lumps of clay or dough, raw material requiring the able fingers of expert educators. Only such a vision could have yielded the schools our children labor in today.

A new vision

If we are to see the current system for what it is, we must have a new vision of what education should be. Education should be seen as a way of encouraging the child's natural curiosity. That change in focus automatically makes the child the active party in the enterprise. (Various educational fads pay lip service to the child as active

4

party, but they do not mean it.) Children come into the world thirsting for knowledge about their surroundings. The educational process needs only to abstain from killing that curiosity. Each child is unique. The last thing he or she needs is a procrustean school. The things that interest politicians and education professionals, such as national standards, are so many distractions.

Contrary to Gilliam, capitalism has a central role in education. Facilitating education involves the provision of products and services. If we have learned anything from the collapse of communism in Eastern Europe and the Soviet Union, it is that nothing can outperform the private economy in the delivery of goods and services. Governments consistently fail in that endeavor because politicians and bureaucrats do not face the same incentives that private businesspeople face. Private enterprise is activity that must attract and please willing customers. Government is force. That difference explains much of what goes on in the world. The choice in education, as in so much else, is between a system that respects people and one that does not. The premise of this book is that people can, and have a right to, run their own lives. They have a right to raise their children. To deny that is folly. If they do not have that ability and right, how could they choose leaders to do it for them? How could there be leaders to choose? Those leaders would suffer the same disabilities as everyone else. The denial of individual liberty and responsibility—and the free society that results from them—is self-refuting.[2]

Culture wars

The public schools have not been of concern only in the academic realm. In the realm of cultural values, they have also caused much turmoil. That is nothing new. Government schools have always been an instrument of political policy—which means they have long been used to deprive a segment of the population its culture or even its language. As Ludwig von Mises wrote, "The main tool of compulsory denationalization and assimilation is education. ... In linguistically mixed territories it turned into a dreadful weapon in the hands of governments determined to change the linguistic allegiance of their subjects."[3]

In the United States, the schools first insulted the Catholics. Later, religionists fought secularists over evolution, a fight that still has not gone away, although the outs are now in and vice versa. Today, the advocates of sex education and condom distribution battle the advocates of abstinence. Those who would pray in school fight with atheists. So-called liberals want *Huckleberry Finn* removed from school libraries, while some fundamentalist Christians are uneasy with *The Wizard of Oz* and *The Diary of Anne Frank*. How can these disputes be resolved without someone's values being shoved down someone else's throat? They cannot. Public schools make those disputes insoluble.

Americans do not appreciate it, but the nations of Europe once had a similar battle over the state church. Horrible sectarian wars were fought between people who felt that unless they imposed their religion on others, the others would impose theirs on them. Then, when civil strife had reached its peak, someone got a great idea: the separation of church and state. Let people choose and finance their own religion and leave government—that is, force—out of it. That idea culminated in the First Amendment to the U.S. Constitution. That doctrine, as much as anything, was responsible for the unprecedented civil harmony that existed in the United States for much of its history.

Today, almost no one in the United States wants a national religion. Yet most people are firmly committed to a national education. Conservatives and statist-liberals, Republicans and Democrats alike, favor uniform national standards for every public school in the nation. What most people do not realize is that national religion and national education involve similar issues and the same threat that someone's ideas will be imposed on others. Auberon Herbert, a libertarian in 19th-century England, saw this clearly when he wrote:

> Whoever fairly faces the question must admit that the same set of arguments which condemns a national religion also condemns a national system of education. It is hard to pronounce sentence on the one and absolve the other. Does a national church compel some to support a system to which they are opposed? So does a national system of education. Does the one exalt the principle of majorities over the individual conscience? So does the other. Does a national church imply a distrust of the people, of their willingness to make sacrifices, of their capacity to manage their own affairs? So does a national system of education. Does the one chill and repress higher meanings and produce formalism? So does the other.

In America, state education is as much out of place as state religion. America's revolution was dedicated to freedom of conscience as well as economic liberty. The limits on government power brought dramatic prosperity. The separation of church and state was a key expression of that limitation. But because of several contradictions in theory and practice, that libertarian revolution was not complete. We need to call a truce in the education wars and to separate school and state so that we may complete the stunted authentic liberal revolution and enjoy its material and spiritual fruits.

The family as educator

If the state does not look after education, who will? Some cannot even imagine an alternative, although we have not always had government schools. As Auberon Herbert noted, "If government half a century ago had provided us all with dinners and breakfasts, it would be the practice of our orators today to assume the impossibility of our providing for ourselves." When people are free, there has been and will be only one answer to the question of who will look after education: the family. The institution of the family is an outgrowth of individualism and freedom. A man and a woman freely choose to build a life together and raise children. The idea of family without primary responsibility for education is ludicrous. As will be discussed later, the public school has been an insidious assault on the integrity of the family. It did not appear that way at first. School districts were small, and schools were local. The schools claimed to value the family. The slow process of centralization and bureaucratization, however, has long removed whatever control families once had over education of their children. To those who say families cannot be trusted with the education of children, the proper answer is: then why do you wish to leave democratic decision making regarding the schools to the heads of those families? Surely it is more feasible for parents to make decisions about their own children's education than it is for them to make such decisions for everyone's children.

A matter of semantics

Throughout the book, the terms "public education," "state education," "national education," "public schools," "state schools," and "government schools" are used interchangeably. Of those terms, "public schools" is the oddest. A private school is open to the public. It is supported by that part of the public that attends. So why don't we call it a public school? Just as Dorothy Gilliam (see above) assumed that the community and the private sector are in opposition, so do people oppose the public and private sectors. My home, of course, is a private place. But what about a restaurant? Clearly, it is a public place—but not in the way that a public school is. What is the difference? The difference is that the restaurant relies on the consent of its customers; the school does not need the consent of its students

7

or those who finance it. "Public" and "private" are therefore misleading labels. We would advance the cause of clear thinking immensely if, instead, we called them the coercive and consensual sectors. The "public" in "public schools" is an Orwellian euphemism for *coercive*. Their money and their students are procured by force. That is not a pretty thought. No wonder the school administrators prefer the word "public." Nevertheless, the term "public school" is established, and this book will use it in the usual way.

A final note: for various reasons, this book will not discuss higher education, although there are many "public" colleges, and government has much to say about the private ones. Suffice it to say that the increase in federal funding and control over the past several decades presents a threat to colleges and universities similar to the one it presents to primary and secondary schools. The lessons from the latter are fully applicable to the former.

There are important differences, however. Attendance at college is not compulsory, of course. Moreover, the young people in primary and secondary schools are much more impressionable than those in the institutions of higher education. That is why the matter with respect to public schools is so urgent. Our children's lives are at stake.

Notes

[1] Quoted from Malthus's *Essay on the Principle of Population* in E. G. West, "The Uneasy Case for State Education," *New Individualist Review*, Winter 1966, p. 48.

[2] This, of course, is a woefully incomplete defense of liberty and individual rights. For a proper philosophical justification for natural rights, see, among others, Ayn Rand, "Man's Rights" in *Capitalism: The Unknown Ideal* (New York: New American Library, 1967); Tibor Machan, *Individuals and Their Rights* (LaSalle, Ill.: Open Court, 1989); and Douglas B. Rasmussen and Douglas J. Den Uyl, *Liberty and Nature: An Aristotelian Defense of Liberal Order* (LaSalle, Ill.: Open Court, 1991).

[3] Ludwig von Mises, *Ominipotent Government: The Rise of the Total State and Total War* (1944; New Rochelle, N.Y.: Arlington House, 1969), p. 82. Elsewhere, Mises wrote that the only way to keep education from having a political character is to keep government out. "The rearing and instruction of youth must be left entirely to parents and to private associations and institutions." *Liberalism: A Socio-Economic Exposition*, trans. Ralph Raico (1962; Kansas City, Mo.: Sheed Andrews and McMeel, 1978), p. 115.

2

What's Wrong
with Public Schools

*It's time to admit that public education operates like a planned economy,
a bureaucratic system in which everybody's role is spelled out in advance and
there are few incentives for innovation and productivity. It's no surprise that
our school system doesn't improve: It more resembles the communist economy
than our own market economy.*

—Albert Shanker
President, American Federation of Teachers

T o have reasonable expectations about the public schools, we
must be clear about what they are and how they operate. It is
necessary to look at how they are funded and controlled and what
implications those aspects of the system have for the service being
provided. It must be stressed that one cannot take the schools as a
given, inquire how they are performing, and then sift through
countless studies to come to a conclusion. The public school system
must be investigated from the inside out. Only then can the performance studies be evaluated intelligently.

Public schools are government schools. That obvious statement
has important implications. Government is the institution that has a
monopoly on the legal use of force in a society. Most significantly,
government obtains its revenue by force—taxation. As government
schools, the public schools are financed entirely out of taxation. Most
school revenue comes from the local taxes on real estate. Owners of
real estate are assessed on the basis of the value of their land and
buildings. The growing federal and state financing of public educa-

tion comes from income taxes. Public education's dependence on taxation is emphasized here because it is the key characteristic of the system. It explains much else about the public schools. And it will enable us to contrast public schooling with its alternative, free-market education (which includes many possibilities, including home schooling).

What does the presence of taxation indicate about the schools? It indicates that those who run the schools have an access to revenue that no one outside of government has. The proprietor of a shoe store cannot send you a bill, whether or not you buy shoes there, and demand payment under penalty of law. He cannot raise prices and compel payment from you whether you are happy about the price increase or not. All he can do is try to attract you to the store and hope that you like the shoes and will freely agree to exchange money for them.

Those who operate the public schools are not nearly as helpless as the shoe-store proprietor. The compulsory funding of schools creates a distinctive attitude in school administrators and teachers that is not found in owners of shoe stores and other private enterprises. The people who come into the shoe store are potential customers, free to walk out without buying. In contrast, the citizens of a school district are taxpayers, who have no choice but to pay their tax bills. Sure, they can move to another jurisdiction. But they face the same compulsion there.

Unsurprisingly, the school authorities treat the taxpayers differently from the way that a shoe-store owner treats his customers. An elected school board official, of course, has his eye on the next election and for that reason must at least appear to be doing things that the voter-taxpayers approve of. Some political theorists presume that the pressure for reelection is similar to the pressures that businessmen face in the marketplace. The similarities, however, do not go far below the surface. Electing a school board official has little in common with picking a shoe store. When shopping for shoes, the customer makes a straightforward decision for himself. He picks the store and buys.

Selecting a school board is very different. No one citizen can decide who serves on the board. If a citizen approves of a particular candidate, he must persuade over 50 percent of his fellow citizens to vote for the same person. His one vote means very little. The margin of victory in most elections is far larger than one vote. The chances of any one person casting the deciding vote are far smaller than the risk of being killed in an auto accident on the way to the polls. Besides that, the average voter has no strong incentive to exert the effort to acquire the knowledge needed to cast an informed vote. That incentive is lacking because people other than himself would get the bulk of any benefits of his effort whether or not *they* exert any effort at all. That is known as the free-rider problem. It plagues all aspects of democracy.

Another problem with administering schools democratically is that the costs of casting a vote are perceived as small by voters. A given voter will pay only a small portion of the expense that his vote might bring about. If he thinks about the monetary cost of his vote at all, he is likely to think only of his small share, not the overall cost. In the marketplace, by contrast, people tend to face the full money costs of their choices. Thus, in the democratic arena there are distortions with respect to individual action that are not found in the marketplace.

Democratic organization of schools presents other problems not found in market organization. What if a citizen shares some but not all of the positions taken by a school board candidate? The electoral system treats his vote for the candidate as unconditional. He has no way to make clear that his endorsement is conditional or partial. He is stuck with a package deal that may look good only in comparison to the other candidates. Again, that problem is solvable in the marketplace. A person can choose to buy only what he likes from a given store and to go elsewhere for other items. In a private education market, parents, if need be, could even send their children to one school to study French and to another for math. The market is the most flexible arrangement for satisfying consumers that can be imagined. It is precisely that flexibility that is missing in bureaucracy, whether controlled democratically or not.

Even if a voter finds a school board candidate he likes, there is, of course, no guarantee that once elected the candidate will do what he promised during the election. What then? Can the people who voted for him sue for misrepresentation? Of course not. They are stuck with their candidate. Sure, they can try to vote him out in the next election. But by then the damage may have been done. And those who are upset with the board member will need to persuade many other people to vote the member out, as well. That cumbersome requirement has no analogue in the market.

The nonmarket organization of education has a serious but unappreciated implication for the financing of schools: people do not know what they pay. As Myron Lieberman writes, "None of us knows the costs of public education, from our own pockets or the government's. These costs are extremely diffuse and intermingled with others beyond identification. Even with the help of a supercomputer, it is impossible to ascertain what any individual is paying for public education."[1]

Generally, it is easy to tell what we pay for the various goods and services we buy. But when every level of government, taxing us in a variety of ways, puts money into the schools, how can anyone know precisely what he has been forced to contribute?

That lack of knowledge has further consequences. Most people will not undergo the arduous effort to find out how much they pay. Many people will shrug and think, "What's the point? I won't be able to do anything about it anyway." That understandable ignorance and weakening of responsibility suit the authorities just fine. They would prefer not to have the taxpayers looking over their shoulders, closely watching their decisions. It gives them substantial rein to spend money and to experiment with any fad in education theory that catches their fancy. The system's inherent lack of accountability insulates the administrators from those who foot the bill and suffer the educational results. It also enables them to form close alliances with education professionals, who are seen as the experts who understand the "science" of education and child development, although there are excellent reasons for believing that those are bogus disciplines.[2]

That mystification of financing creates fertile ground for bureaucratic irresponsibility. As noted in the Appendix, the financing of public schools has skyrocketed in recent years. It is unlikely that the taxpayers have even been aware of that fact. The system has been arranged to keep taxpayers in the dark. No, they are not prohibited from acquiring the information. But such acquisition is made so difficult that most people, busy as they are raising their families and making a living, will not have the time to navigate the backwaters of the bureaucracy. The division of labor, normally a blessing, is perverted so as to discourage people from exercising self-responsibility.

A related problem is that tax financing precludes market prices for educational services. Market prices do not only let buyers know what they are paying. They are the fruit of a complex communications process that encapsulates information about the relative scarcity of resources and conveys it to all participants in the marketplace. That information is crucial to intelligent planning by buyers and producers of services. It is at the very heart of market competition, which Nobel-laureate F. A. Hayek properly called a "discovery procedure."

We live in a world of uncertainty, an open-ended world in which perfect knowledge is denied us. Discovery of new things and

14

methods is always possible. But discovery is fueled by incentives. As economist Israel M. Kirzner points out, in the marketplace, the lure of profit creates incentives for entrepreneurs to find unsatisfied needs and to devise ways of satisfying them. Those incentives do not exist in government schools.

In the market, entrepreneurs are accountable to consumers; they face the constant threat of financial loss. The alleged accountability of officeholders to voters is a mirage. It bears no real resemblance to the accountability of the marketplace. If the shoe-store operator misrepresents his product, there is recourse in the civil courts. Offended customers can take their business elsewhere without notice. They do not have to persuade over 50 percent of the other customers to join in a boycott. That power held by the individual consumer in the marketplace—sometimes called consumer sovereignty—is lacking in the democratic administration of services such as education.

The inherent insulation of school boards (and other democratic bodies) from real accountability aggravates a phenomenon known as the Iron Law of Oligarchy. The law says that in almost any group endeavor, a small elite will emerge as the most active in determining the activities of the group. Even in a neighborhood bridge club, two or three people will show the most interest in running the group— finding a place to play, determining the game night, and so forth. The Iron Law asserts itself because people tend to have busy lives, and few will find the activity of such importance that they wish to invest an extraordinary amount of time. Of course, in a bridge club the Iron Law is benign. But that is not true with things such as school boards. Even if people might like to spend lots of time studying every aspect of the school system, attending board meetings, and the like, most simply cannot do it. Besides, as mentioned above, the return on the effort will seem too small. Those who can invest such time usually have a special interest in doing so—members of the teachers' union, for example. In the end, school policy will be inordinately influenced by a small group of activists, not by the mass of taxpayers or parents.

Democracy equals bureaucracy

John E. Chubb and Terry M. Moe, in their book *Politics, Markets & America's Schools*, argue persuasively that the problem with the public schools is precisely their democratic organization. It is not that democracy has malfunctioned in the running of schools, they write. On the contrary, it has functioned as it has been meant to function. "Our reasoning is that much of [the bureaucratization of the schools] is an inevitable and logical consequence of the direct democratic control of schools," write Chubb and Moe.[3] Elsewhere in the book, they write, "Democracy is essentially coercive. The winners get to use public authority to impose their policies on the losers."[4] They zero in on the bureaucratization of public schools. To be sure, education bureaucrats work hard to advance their own interests.

> As public officials, they [the school bureaucrats] have incentives to expand their budgets, programmatic authority, and administrative controls. These are the basics of bureaucratic well-being, and their pursuit is an integral part of the job. Bureaucrats also belong to important interest groups—of administrators, of education "professionals"—that lobby government from the outside (ostensibly) as well. Although traditionally they have tried to portray themselves as nonpolitical experts pursuing the great good, they are in fact a powerful constellation of special interests dedicated to hierarchical control and the formalization of education.[5]

But the impetus toward bureaucratization does not come only from the bureaucrats. It is systemic. As Chubb and Moe note:

> Institutions of democratic control are inherently destructive of school autonomy and inherently conducive to bureaucracy. This happens because of the way all the major participants—politicians, interest groups, bureaucrats—are motivated and empowered by their institutional setting to play the game of structural politics. . . . Schools, we believe, are the products of their institutional settings.[6]

Their book is a persuasive case against democracy in education. Its thesis can be summed up in a syllogism: democratic control leads to bureaucracy; bureaucracy destroys schools; thus democratic control destroys schools. Public schools did not always seem so bureaucratic. They have changed over the decades in some obvious ways. There is far more centralization today. In 1945–46, there were over 100,000 school districts in the United States. In 1980–81, there were fewer than 16,000.[7] While the teacher population of the public schools increased 57 percent between 1960 and 1984, and the number of principals and supervisors increased by 79 percent, other personnel skyrocketed by 500 percent. Meanwhile, pupil enrollment rose a mere 9 percent during that period.[8] Districts are far larger, diluting even further the influence of any single voter and concentrating the power of bureaucrats who are more insulated than ever before. Another form of centralization has come from the organization of teachers into national unions; that process grew rapidly in the 1960s. Economist Sam Peltzman of the University of Chicago notes that student achievement deteriorated most where unionization succeeded earliest, most likely because "union-style job security and a flexible ability to replace underperforming teachers can not always co-exist."[9]

Centralization has been intensified by the fact that funding is more and more coming from the state and federal governments, moving control of the purse strings further away from the people forced to use the schools. In 1960, local governments provided 60 percent of school funding. By 1987, the percentage had fallen to 43.9.[10] That trend continues apace. In Michigan, state officials have dumped the local property tax for school financing in favor of the state's sales tax. Other states are on the verge of following Michigan. The move away from the local property tax is being fueled by the egalitarian complaint that areas with higher property values can spend more on schools than areas with lower property values.[11] (More on that below.)

The cause of centralization is being pursued with a vengeance by both Democrats and Republicans, who favor national goals and standards to which each state's public schools would have to conform (at least if they want to receive federal money). President Clinton is pushing a plan that would let the states disband local school boards that do not fulfill federal requirements. His "Improving America's School Act" comes on top of the "Goals 2000: Educate America Act," initiated by President Bush, which prescribes national standards based on the vague "outcome-based education" approach and provides more federal money, especially to poor school districts.[12]

Thus, the old, semi-plausible federalist theory that the states were to be laboratories free to experiment and innovate is casually tossed onto the landfill. Democratic control on a small, local, face-to-face scale, while still inferior to the marketplace, suffers fewer evils than democratic control on a large scale. The school board in a tiny burg is run by neighbors and is bound to be less bureaucratic than the consolidated mega-districts of today.

The results of centralization were not merely academic. As David and Micki Colfax write:

Within a decade [of the launching of the Russian satellite Sputnik in 1957] local control of school districts was transferred, primarily because of changes in funding, to state and federal agencies. Sputnik had, in effect, transformed American education into a centralized system in which organizational men and women—administrators and bureaucrats—rather than teachers and students, became the key players in a very big, very expensive game. It is a legacy which haunts and poisons the classroom a generation later. . . . With the increased power accorded the education bureaucrats following passage of the Elementary and Secondary Education Act in the mid-sixties, curriculum, content, and, perhaps most importantly, the teacher's authority and autonomy in the classroom underwent significant transformations. It was becoming increasingly difficult to be a teacher in an era in which uniformity, compliance, and administrative control were in ascendance. And if it was becoming increasingly difficult to be a good teacher, it was clearly more difficult to obtain a first-rate education in the typical American school.[13]

Parents versus nonparents

So far we have addressed only compulsory support of the schools. Let's now distinguish between those citizens with school-aged children and those without. The public school system does not care about that distinction. Both sets of people are treated the same. Bachelors and the elderly pay as much as parents of children and teenagers. Is there justice in that? Advocates of public schools defend that practice by saying that education is a "public good." The argument says that since everyone benefits from the betterment of society that comes from educating the young, everyone should pay for that education.

What is wrong with that argument? The premise is not wrong. In a sense, we all tend to benefit from other people's being educated. We benefit from the fact that educated people will likely expand the range of goods and services offered us. But of course, we will pay for those things. There is no free ride. For that reason, those are not the benefits that school taxes are designed to compensate for. The advocates of school taxes have more general benefits in mind. And, again, it cannot be denied that there are general benefits from living in an educated community. We could point out that in a free society, people are supposed to decide for themselves how much they value things and therefore should not be compelled to finance someone else's well-being. But we can let that point go for now. The tax

18

advocates' point is off the mark for another reason: we benefit every day from things that others do for themselves and no one advocates that we pay taxes to offset the cost.

Reading is a form of education. If an educated community creates general benefits, so does a well-read community. But no one but a full-blown socialist would advocate using the taxing power to produce books for the public and run book stores (though they do favor public libraries). Other activities also benefit the community generally: cleanliness, politeness, attractive clothing, and more. Should people be taxed to provide those things?

Underlying the public-goods theory of school financing is the premise that if the alleged "free riders" do not help finance education, too little education will be purchased. But it strains credulity to assert that if the public is not taxed to support the schools, people will buy too little education. People buy education because they expect to benefit themselves or their children in material as well as nonmaterial ways. They are not likely to forgo education because the public will be getting amorphous free benefits.

The tax advocates do not know what the "right" amount of education is. So they cannot claim to know that less than that amount will be purchased in the absence of school taxes. Perhaps "too much" education will be purchased if the tax system is used to subsidize it. How can the tax advocates deny that?

Education does not have the defining characteristics of a public good as found in standard economic theory. (Much criticism can be made of that theory. But let's accept it for the sake of argument.) Standard theory anticipates "market failure" in the production of goods for which exclusion of nonpayers is exceedingly difficult or impossible, and consumption by one person does not diminish the good for others. For example, a classic (alleged) public good is a lighthouse. Economists for many years have argued that the market will not produce lighthouses, at least not in the "right" amount, because it is impossible to charge every ship that is guided by the light and because one ship's use of the light does not dim the beam for anyone else. In other words, there will be free riders, and the marginal cost of production is zero. Now, it so happens that lighthouses in England were privately and profitably operated for over a hundred years, as Nobel-laureate Ronald Coase discovered in 1973.[14] But that aside, what has public-goods theory to do with education? First, it is obviously easy to exclude nonpayers from receiving the service. Potential free riders can be barred from entering the schools. Second, at least at some point, the admission of an additional student will diminish the service for students already there. An additional student will make the class more crowded, will require more text-books and other scarce materials, and will subtract the teacher's attention from other students.

Thus, education does not have public-goods characteristics, and public-goods theory cannot be used to justify taxation to support the schools. On the contrary, in its fundamental properties, formal education is like many other normal goods and services. True, many people judge education to be more important than other things offered on the market. But the same can be said for food, shelter, clothing, and medical care. That does not justify nonmarket provision—especially when nonmarket provision is demonstrably inferior to market provision.

Schools and the family

Chubb and Moe make an unappreciated point about the democratic control of schools. Since it may not distinguish between parents and nonparents (all taxpayers must have an equal standing, theoretically), the people with the most stake in the success of the system have no more say over it than those with little or no stake. They write:

> The fundamental point to be made about parents and students is not that they are politically weak, but that, even in a perfectly functioning democratic system, the public schools are not meant to be theirs to control and are literally not supposed to provide them with the kind of education they might want. The schools are agencies of society as a whole, and everyone has a right to participate in their governance. Parents and students have a right to participate too. But they have no right to win. In the end, they have to take what society gives them.[15]

Parents and children are stuck with the education that someone else gives them. (As noted above, it is not *society* that determines what they get. Rather, it is the subgroup that is most motivated and best skilled at taking control of the system.) So-called public education, thus, is exposed as an insidious assault on parents and their children, that is, on the family. That is ironic, indeed, since much research, for example the work done for many years by James Coleman, strongly suggests that the real difference between effective education and ineffective education is the condition of families. In other words, educational "inputs"—such as money, teacher-student ratios, and so on—are not as important for the success of a child's education as an active, supportive family. Yet public schools have the effect of

20

reducing the influence of the family. In general, the existence of public schools, which make so many important decisions in the lives of children, tells parents, "You don't have to worry about your child's schooling. That is in the hands of the experts." If parents do not have to select a school and explicitly pay for it, many will not be as closely involved in their children's education as they otherwise would be. The public school authorities pay lip service to parental involvement. They want the parents to encourage their children to do their homework and to attend class. But they do not want parents involved in the big decisions, such as where their children go to school or what sort of instruction they should receive. What the authorities want from parents is blind support.

Let's look closely at how public schooling subverts the family. We should begin by noting that education is one of the most important things that parents give their children. I am using the term "education" in its broadest sense; it includes moral as well as academic matters. It also includes formal schooling, though it need not. To transfer responsibility for formal education from parents to the state is a substantial blow to the institution of the family, which, as nearly everyone today acknowledges, is critical to the formation of good character in children.

Public schools necessarily transfer from parents to government the very decision of what schools children will attend. Compulsory attendance laws require that all children go to school. The first consequence of those laws is that the government claims the power to say what is and is not a school. Its own schools, of course, qualify. The courts over the years have upheld the right of parents to send their children to private schools or to home-school them. But the government nevertheless retains the power to disqualify schools and even the parents themselves (in the case of homeschooling) if its standards are not met.

The government even dictates which public schools children may attend. True, parents can choose a school by buying a home in a particular neighborhood. But that is a weak method of preserving the right to make an important decision. The choice of where to live is influenced by many other factors—job, home prices, other amenities, and so on—besides schools. But even if it were not, the location of one's home may have little to do with what school one's children attend. School districts can redraw boundaries at any time or institute busing. Either of these decisions can wreck a homebuying decision overnight. Many people have selected homes because they liked the neighborhood school, only to see that choice nullified by an arbitrary decision of the school board or a judge.

21

Parents can choose the school their children will attend by selecting a private school. But as noted above, they must pay school taxes even if they do not use the government schools. That fact obviously limits who can buy private education. Middle- and lower-income people usually cannot afford to pay for both public and private schooling. So for many, the choice of a private school is purely theoretical. It offers no safeguard against government control over this most important area of childraising.[16]

By determining the schools that one's children attend, the government also influences with whom one's children associate. If parents believe that students in their child's school engage in behavior that they would not want their child to engage in, they do not have the power to switch to another school. Many parents in the inner cities surely would like to remove their children from schools in which students carry guns and knives, commit violence, or use drugs and alcohol. They are virtually powerless to place their children in a better situation. By taking this matter out of the parents' hands, the government asserts its prerogative over parents in the matter of childrearing. The government is effectively saying to parents that *it* knows better than they how to bring up their children. Parents are expected to take responsibility for raising their children, but their power and authority to do so are badly undermined by government.

That denial of authority is manifest in other ways. Parents have next to nothing to say about the values taught at the school to which the government assigns their children. As noted above, the much-touted power of democracy means almost nothing. If the school district adopts a values curriculum or program to which a parent objects, such as, to take the latest fashion, a compulsory community-service requirement, there is little he or she can do. It is likely not within a parent's means to launch a campaign to change the school board. If enough parents are outraged, a successful protest may be possible. But what if the curriculum strongly bothers only a few parents and not the others? Why should the few have no choice but to accept what the school board adopts and what the majority of parents acquiesces in? For those few parents, an important part of raising their children has been taken from their hands and given to elected officials and their appointed bureaucrats. (By the way, community compulsory service patently violates the 13th Amendment's prohibition of involuntary servitude.)

Values permeate education. If honest effort is praised and cheating penalized, a particular moral view of the world is conveyed. If honesty and dishonesty are equally "tolerated," another moral view is conveyed. Value-free education is a chimera. Even an attempt to divorce values from education conveys a view of values: that they are unimportant. Surgeon General Joycelyn Elders and others mock the idea of value-laden education as something only Christian fundamentalists care about. In a survey of future teachers at an elite school of education, 88 percent said they would prefer to teach a course in moral education in which students were taught that there were no right answers to moral questons rather than to teach a course that taught such virtues as courage, justice, self-control, and honesty.[17] But fundamentalists surely are not the only people who want their children to learn values. By their own example, most parents teach their children that productiveness, self-responsibility, self-discipline, courage, and justice are good things. They would certainly want their children's education to convey those virtues. It is reasonable to be wary of the teaching of values in government schools. The appropriate policy, however, is to scrap the government schools, not the idea of value-laden education. Government schools necessarily interfere with the parents' right to direct their children's moral education.

Despite the claim of moral neutrality, public education is linked to a particular set of values, namely, the values of the modern welfare, or social-service, state. Those values include moral agnosticism (erroneously called tolerance), government activism, egalitarianism, "welfare rights" to taxpayer largess, collectivism, and a watered-down version of socialism that looks much like the economic theory of the 1930s known as fascism. Those values are communicated in history lessons that portray the private marketplace as greedy and callous, and the government as enlightened and kind. The worldview promulgated in many public school systems includes a notion of personal morality symbolized by the dispensing of condoms to teenagers—without parental permission—in the name of "safe sex." Those who control the curricula operate under the illusion that sex can be discussed value-free—and that only the matter of teenage abstinence ventures into the forbidden territory of morality. Nearly every form of so-called diversity and multiculturalism—in reality, cultural and moral relativism—has a place in the public schools. But diversity is a qualified value. It does not extend to the view, which some parents may wish to have incorporated into the children's education, that cultures that prize reason and enterprise are better than those that do not. Nor does it extend to what may be called the individualist and procapitalist values of America's revolutionary heritage.

The values of the environmental movement are fully incorporated into the public school curricula. Children are taught that recycling is an unconditional virtue. The possibility that recycling has a cost is not even considered. Most students would not know, for example, that recycling materials requires the use of other resources and that the value of the resources used may outweigh the value of those saved. For example, paper recycling requires vehicles burning gasoline to pick up and deliver the newspapers to the recycling centers. To recycle newspapers, they have to be de-inked. But that creates a toxic sludge that has to be disposed of. Those facts are rarely brought up. Instead, children learn that if we do not recycle, there will be no room to dispose of trash and eventually no room to live. The facts are otherwise, but somehow those facts also do not find their way into most classrooms.

It is a rare class indeed that studies how free markets deal with resources. In the name of environmental awareness, children are taught that business wantonly destroys rain forests, dirties the air, kills whales and dolphins, poisons us with pesticides, and pollutes the soil and waters with radioactive material. It is highly unlikely that many children have heard of the "tragedy of the commons." That is the name for the problems that occur when ownership of a resource is not permitted. It was recognized by Adam Smith, but was given its name by Garrett Hardin, the environmentalist. Smith understood that a resource that anyone may use but no one may own will be depleted, because no one will have an incentive to husband the resource. Any benefits from such activity might be seized by someone else. Ownership secured by the legal system—that is, private property—provides an incentive for people to maximize the value of resources far into the future. Many environmental problems have their roots in the government's policy of prohibiting private ownership, for instance in air space and bodies of water. But students are not likely to learn that.

The invasion of the schools by environmentalism is intended to influence children from an early age with a pagan-style worship of Mother Earth. The environmental movement has succeeded in shaping the curriculum for most children. Teachers are bombarded with materials arguing that capitalism will destroy the planet unless government is given substantial new powers. That effort also influences parents. Procter and Gamble took a survey a few years ago to learn where adults get their information about the environment. The news media placed second in the survey. First place went to schoolchildren. Children are relaying to their parents environmental information that comes, via the school, from the environmental movement itself. But that information is dressed up as value-free, scientific, uncontroversial education. Thus, when local governments compel recycling of trash under threat of legal penalties, few people object.

Another set of values that are imposed on children in public schools could be called the New Puritanism. The misconceived war on drugs has spawned an attitude, pushed hard in the schools, that even minor indulgences are bad. Children are taught that drugs, tobacco, and alcohol are ill-advised not only for them but also for their parents. They are pressured to take pledges promising not to drink alcohol. When my daughter Jennifer started public school, she had to sign a form acknowledging that she would be expelled from school if she sold drugs. A parent drinking a beer after work could find his child condemning him for doing something evil. There have been instances where teachers have encouraged children to describe the drinking practices of their parents in the name of "helping" them. In some cases, students are pushed into informing on their parents. In Maryland recently, a young girl turned her parents in to the police for growing marijuana at home. She learned to do that in a school antidrug program.[18] Collusion between the schools and child-welfare agencies has led to an outbreak of dubious child-abuse charges. Teaching children to be suspicious of their parents has an obvious corrosive effect on the family.[19]

School and the Therapeutic State

The union of the school system and the medical profession, which is implicit in the drug and child-abuse issues, has yielded perhaps the most absurd phenomenon of all: the legal drugging of children because they do not pay attention in class. This is Huxley's *Brave New World* in all its naked horror. The young son of a friend of mine was diagnosed by a school official as having attention deficit disorder (ADD) and was prescribed the powerful drug Ritalin. That diagnosis was made after a 16-minute observation of the child in class, during which he was said to have paid attention only (!) 41 percent of the time the teacher was reading a story aloud. Is any comment really necessary? Only the education establishment in league with psychiatry could decide that a child's restlessness in class is a disorder, most likely of genetic origin. Children, in the establishment's view, are supposed to be docile for hours while an adult drones on about something that may or may not interest anyone else. They are supposed to accept that they may not go to the bathroom or get a drink of water or even speak without permission. And any child who cannot live up to that modest set of requirements must be suffering from a disease that only a powerful drug can cure. That is what government schools have brought us. ADD is one of the latest diagnoses from what Thomas Szasz calls the Therapeutic State, the alliance of government and medicine, which proclaims that problems of living are, in fact, illnesses. (Dyslexia and other "learning disabilities" have a similar dubious scientific foundation, writes retired pediatric neurologist Fred A. Baughman, Jr.[20]) Control of our children—not to mention big bucks for the "special ed" profession—is a key objective on the Therapeutic State's agenda. In a recent article about the converse of ADD, High Sensitivity (otherwise known as shyness!), Hillel Schwartz writes:

> Instead of examining our social, political, economic and educational institutions when confronted with problems of noise, intolerance, underachievement and inability to focus, we relegate these problems to individual and *inborn* traits from whose lifelong tentacles we may perhaps be released once our human geneticists have gotten up to speed.[21]

The cult of conformity

The public schools pride themselves on teaching good citizenship. But that deserves a closer look. "Good citizenship" turns out to mean allegiance to the government and its policies. Jennifer was in first grade during the prelude to the U.S. war against Iraq. She was fed the government's line that Desert Shield and Desert Storm were defensive measures and told to wear an American flag pin each day.

For all the talk of diversity, a fundamental conformity pervades the school. Dissent, at least in important things, is not encouraged. Parents who object to the dominant values and who wish to give their young children a firm foundation based on their own philosophy are out of luck. Defenders of the public schools say that it is good for children to encounter diverse views; it is said to be important to the development of critical thinking. That objection misses its target. To be sure, people benefit from new information and divergent views. Even if a person is not persuaded to the new view, he will understand his own position better for having considered a conflicting position. As John Stuart Mill wrote in *On Liberty*, "He who knows only his own side of the case, knows little of that."

But using the schools to circumvent parents' right to control their children's upbringing has nothing to do with teaching critical thinking, which is not really taught in the schools anyway. All it does is impose an authority on children possibly in violation of the parent's convictions. Children encounter views different from those held by parents without any help from schools. They spend time with other children; they watch television; they have brothers and sisters who have friends. In most homes, children will have little difficulty hearing diverse opinions. That is not the issue. The issue is, who should have the ultimate control over whom children associate with, the state or the parents? In a free society, there is only one answer.

The invocation of critical thinking serves to hide the indoctrination function of the public schools. The economist John R. Lott, Jr., has written that the public schools were established not because children would go uneducated, but rather because they would otherwise receive the "wrong" kind of education. In his view, the governing elite needs the schools to create public support for the state's activities. Since all government activity consists in the transfer of wealth from those who produced it to those who did not, such activity has the potential to create its own resistance. Those with a stake in the transfer activity have a clear interest in fostering a favorable consensus. As Lott put it:

> One possible method of lowering the cost of transfer payments is to instill certain ideological beliefs—for example, the perceived legitimacy of existing transfers. If individuals believe that the government is "fair" and "legitimate," the costs of undertaking government actions are reduced. . . . The higher the level of transfers, the greater the opposition and thus the greater return to indoctrination.[22]

Lott's theory has important implications. If public schools are intended to create favorable views toward government in the present, they need to create favorable views toward the government's past. Thus, it is unsurprising that the public schools' history curricula cast a favorable light on the periods in which government, particularly the federal government, accumulated unprecedented powers, such as the Progressive Era, the New Deal, and the two world wars. The public schools would have little use for a textbook that presented those watersheds as inimical to the freedom and well-being of society. Moreover, the purchasing clout of large, centralized school districts makes the potential market for any maverick textbook so small that publishers will rarely find such a publication financially worthwhile.

No malevolent conspiracy theory is required to grasp the indoctrination role of the public schools. The eminent journalist Walter Lippmann recognized as early as the 1920s that in a democratic system, government would use propaganda for the "manufacture of consent."[23] Even assuming benign intentions, one can see how the governing class would wish to shape the consensus to accord with its view of the good of the nation (and undoubtedly with the requirements of its continued authority). The schools would naturally play a major role in that process. If the reader still harbors doubts about the propagandist role of the schools, they should be dispelled by education critic Richard Mitchell:

> Imagine that you are one of those functionaries of government in whom there has grown, it seems inescapable, the propensity to command, in however oblique a fashion and for whatever supposedly good purpose, the liberty and property of your constituents. Which would you prefer, educated constituents or ignorant ones? . . . Which would you rather face, even considering your own convictions that the cause in which you want to command liberty and property is just—citizens *with* or *without* the power of informed discretion? Citizens having that power will require of you a laborious and detailed justification of your intentions and expectations and may, even having that, adduce other information and exercise further discretion to the contrary of your propensities. On the other hand, the ill-informed and undiscriminating can easily be persuaded by the recitation of popular slogans and the appeal to self-interest, however spurious. It is only informed discretion that can detect such maneuvers.[24]

Since the schools do not encourage what Mitchell calls "informed discretion," conscientious parents are likely to have a conflict with the academic approach of the public schools. Their authority is further undermined by that conflict. When Jennifer, an early reader, was in first grade, her teacher did not want her to read or do arithmetic above her class level, although she was capable of doing both. She urged my wife and me not to carry out our own view of a proper education, which was to allow and encourage Jennifer to work at as advanced a level as she could and wished to. Despite all the talk about family support being needed for the schools to work, this teacher was telling us to "butt out." The teacher, who boasted a master's degree in reading, explained that kids enjoy reading simpler stories more than more difficult ones (not true of Jennifer) and that the class would soon learn arithmetic with the help of calculators. Calculators! In first grade! I figured that this is the arithmetic equivalent of the look-say method.[25] We had an irreconcilable clash with the school system. We could either give in or pull Jennifer out of school at the end of the year. We pulled her out of school. She, along with sister Emily and brother Ben, has been homeschooled ever since.

The clash with the family is related to another problem created by government schools: the clash with individuality. Despite apparent attempts to grapple with individuality (such as "gifted" programs), the public schools are essentially a one-size-fits-all system. In first grade, advanced readers are mixed with nonreaders. The talented are held back. When reforms are proposed, there are voices warning that too much attention is being given to the brightest children. "Fairness" seems to dictate that the best not get too far ahead. As Murray N. Rothbard writes:

> Some children are dull and demand a slower learning pace; bright children require a rapid pace to develop their faculties. Furthermore, many children are apt in one subject and quite inept in another. They should be permitted to develop themselves in their best subjects and drop the poor ones. Whatever educational standards are imposed from outside, injustice is done to all—to the less able who cannot absorb any instruction, to those with different sets of aptitudes in different subjects, to the bright children whose minds would like to be off and winging in more advanced courses. Similarly, whatever pace the teacher sets in class is bound to be injurious to almost all—to the dull who cannot keep up and to the bright who lose interest. Moreover, those in the middle, the "average," are not always the same in all classes and often are not the same from day-to-day in one class.[26]

Here is a subject that people wish to avoid these days. A misconception of the idea of equality has led many people to eschew the idea that individuals differ in their talents, intelligence, energy, ambition, and so forth. There is a widely held assumption that children are essentially the same and would appear the same if only they were guaranteed equal school facilities. Thus, if some children achieve less than others, that is thought to be a sign of unfairness. When confronted with the palpable failure of the public schools, they reject the private competition alternative—because it cannot guarantee "equality"—and call for greater taxpayer funds for the schools. They go even further and propose transferring money from the wealthier school districts to the poorer school districts. Indeed, for the egalitarians, it is not enough to try to raise the lower levels; the higher levels must be lowered. Jonathan Kozol, one of those egalitarians, writes, "Equity, after all, does not mean simply equal funding. Equal funding for unequal needs is not equality."[27] He goes on to say that simply giving more money to poor districts would not accomplish his egalitarian goal: "Since every district is competing for the same restricted pool of gifted teachers, the "minimum" assured to every district is immediately devalued by the district that can add $10,000 more to teacher salaries. . . . The poorest districts are left where they were before the minimum existed."[28]

Unlike others in his camp, he wishes to keep the property tax as the main support of the public schools. (The sales tax is regressive.) He wants the money to go to a central pool and "equally" distributed to all districts in a state. That way, the money will be transferred from rich to poor. He counsels his allies not to try to fool wealthier people by shrouding that transfer:

> No matter what devices are contrived to bring about equality, it is clear that they require money-transfer, and the largest source of money is the portion of the population that possesses the *most* money. When wealthy districts indicate they see the hand of Robin Hood in this, they are clear-sighted and correct. [Emphasis in orginal.][29]

There are two issues mixed up here. Unquestionably, the inner-city children have been cruelly condemned by government to what are called schools. As Thomas Sowell has said, there are better automobiles in the ghettos than schools. Equally certain is that abolishing the public schools and allowing the free market to provide education would make better schooling available to those children. But that does not mean that bad government schools are the only thing that stand in the way of perfect equality. When Thomas Jefferson wrote that "all men are created equal," he meant it in only one sense: they are born equal in their moral entitlement to life, liberty, and the pursuit of happiness. He certainly did not mean that everyone was equal in musical ability, or mathematical capability, or even in abstract reasoning. We could not all be top rocket scientists if only we were given the same education and supportive environment. We may not know why some people are better suited to particular vocations than others, but we know that it is so.

Variation is the rule among the living. Human beings differ widely in their internal physical makeup. As the biochemist Roger J. Williams has written:

Different human brains are as unlike each other as are the brains of different species and even different orders of animals. . . . Your brain probably differs from your neighbor's far more than your facial features vary from his. . . . Experts agree that every individual tends to have a pattern of mental abilities or potentialities which is distinctive for him or her alone.[30]

Thus, equality of outcomes is a chimera, an impossibility, because of the fundamental differences of individuals. We should no more expect equality of outcomes than we expect people's fingerprints to be the same. Nor should we long for equality in any except the Jeffersonian sense. "Enthusiasm for equality should actually be viewed as anti-human," writes Rothbard. "It tends to repress the flowering of individual personality and diversity and, indeed, of civilization itself."[31]

When confronted with these facts, some people, including some conservatives, retreat to a defense of "equal opportunity." We cannot guarantee equal results, they say, but we should guarantee equal opportunity. The schools are said to be an important factor in that guarantee.

But the new principle is as doomed as the first. How can there really be equal opportunity given the differences among families and the values they inculcate in children and the variation among individuals? Does the child whose parents shun hard work and responsibility have exactly the same opportunity for success as one whose parents teach those virtues by example? Does someone lacking an aptitude for mathematics have the same opportunity that Einstein had to become a great scientist? Hardly. Does the child of parents who have no musical talent have the same opportunity to become a musician as the child of a world-renowned violinist? How could we equalize the opportunity? Should a talent scout be compelled to give the first child the same chance as the second, even though in his wish to economize his time, he may pass over the first for an audition for the second?

The schools' pursuit of equality is bound up with the new "feel good" curriculum, the point of which is ostensibly to instill self-esteem in students. That is what government education has turned to now that it has virtually given up reading, writing, and arithmetic. But it should be obvious that self-esteem cannot be taught or instilled directly. It is the internal reward one earns from real accomplishment.

There is only one proper notion of equal opportunity: the absence of legal barriers to freedom of action. Jim Crow laws and apartheid are examples of government policies that deny people opportunity; those policies made peaceful actions by certain groups of people illegal. Thus those policies violated their rights. But any government action that transfers wealth from those who have earned it to others cannot be defended in the name of equality. Since it violates the rights of those whose property is taken, such policies violate the Jeffersonian notion of equality: equality, that is, before the law. Ironically, the public schools violate the liberty of poor people and deny them freedom to pursue opportunities by taxing them and forcing their children to go to bad schools. Those policies should be ended, not in the name of equality, but in the name of liberty and decency.

In summary, public schools, with their compulsory attendance laws, strike a fundamental blow at the family as the unit of childrearing and at individuality. Many important decisions are transferred from parents and children to government officials, including teachers. Everyone today bemoans the condition of the family. Everyone believes it has something to do with the lack of civility and the depravity of modern society. The most talked-about sources of that condition are welfare, television violence, and video games. But little thought has been given to how the public schools contribute to the weakening of the family. The government school, which most children must attend, is set up as a subtle rival of the family, which cannot even decide to take a vacation between September and June. Charles Murray has pointed out that communities wither when their functions are usurped. The same can be said of families. As the government, through its schools, has taken on more and more of the family's traditional functions, and moved those functions further away, the family to some extent has been drained of its vitality and reason for being. State schools remove the education function from the family. The state commands the parents to send the children to school. The state, not the parents, chooses which school children attend. That schooling is represented as free. What is free is valued less than what one chooses to pay for. All of that adds up to a dilution of the moral authority and functions of the family.[32] The fundamental issue is who raises the children and sees to their education: the state or the parents? In a free society, there can be only one answer. The upshot is that the way to begin revitalizing the family is to abolish the government's schools.

In Chapter 5 we will speculate on what education and the free family might look like in the absence of government schooling. In the next chapter we take a look back to discover why public schools exist.

Notes

[1] Myron Lieberman, *Public Education: An Autopsy* (Cambridge, Mass.: Harvard University Press, 1993), p. 139.

[2] For fascinating explorations of this matter, see the many works of John Holt and Richard Mitchell. The latest in a long series of fads is "outcome-based education." While not exactly definable, it has yielded such injunctions as "focus on what students learn, not on what is taught." And there is this rather vague vision: "The classroom of tomorrow might focus more on drawing out existing abilities than on precisely measuring a student's success with imposed skills; encourage the personal construction of categories rather than impose existing categorical systems; and emphasize individual, personal solutions of an environmental challenge—even if inefficient—more than the efficient group manipulation of symbols that merely represent the solution." Quoted in Paul Greenberg, "Seeking Enlightenment in Educantoland," *The Washington Times*, February 5, 1994, D1. One need not accept the traditional approach to education, in which children are expected to passively receive learning from teachers in a classroom, to see that there is a difference between achievement and phony procedures intended to make children "feel good about themselves." On the coercive and Orwellian nature of outcome-based education (OBE), see Marshall Fritz, "Why OBE and the Traditionalists Are Both Wrong, *Journal of the Association for Supervision and Curriculum Development*, March 1994.

[3] John E. Chubb and Terry M. Moe, *Politics, Markets and America's Schools* (Washington, D.C.: Brookings Institution, 1990), p. 183.

[4] Ibid., p. 28.

[5] Ibid., p. 46.

[6] Ibid., pp. 47, 67.

[7] David Boaz, ed., *Liberating Schools: Education in the Inner City* (Washington, D.C.: Cato Institute, 1991), p. 14.

[8] Boaz, p. 15.

[9] Sam Peltzman, "What's Behind the Decline of the Public Schools," *USA Today Magazine*, March 1994, p. 23. Education critic John Holt blamed the decline in part on "non-intellectual or even anti-intellectual lower middle-class" people who entered teaching as a civil service job in major cities. See Holt, *The Underachieving School* (New York: Delta, 1969), p. 151.

[10] Boaz, p. 15.

[11] This is no defense of property taxes. But Milton Friedman has argued that suburbanites have used the property tax as a way of deducting what would otherwise be nondeductible tuition from their federal income taxes. Allowing all tuition to be deducted would remove that disparity.

[12] Robert Holland, "Stealth Takeover of Education?" *The Washington Times*, February 8, 1994, p. A16. The Goals 2000 legislation was approved by the U.S. Senate in February 1994.

[13] David and Micki Colfax, *Homeschooling for Excellence* (New York: Warner Books), pp. 16, 18. Micki Colfax was a public school teacher who, with her husband, a university professor, took up homeschooling after moving to an isolated farm. Their three sons later attended Harvard University.

[14] Coase's landmark paper, "The Lighthouse in Economics," is reprinted in Tyler Cowen, ed., *The Theory of Market Failure* (Fairfax, Va.: George Mason University Press/Cato Institute, 1988).

[15] Chubb and Moe, p. 32.

[16] "School choice" is supposed to solve that problem by letting parents use some of the money collected by the government to pay tuition at private schools. Problems with that reform will be discussed later.

[17] Charles L. Glenn and Joshua Glenn, "Schooling for Virtue," *First Things*, August/September 1993, p. 45.

[18] Those programs are uninterested in the real pharmacological effects of illegal drugs. Their mission is to have children from a young age unquestioningly accept the government's war on drugs. To see why that war is not what it seems, consult Thomas Szasz, *Ceremonial Chemistry: The Ritual Persecution of Drugs, Addicts, and Pushers* (Garden City, N.Y.: Anchor Books, 1975) and *Our Right to Drugs: The Case for the Free Market* (New York: Praeger, 1992).

[19] See "Kids, Cops and Caseworkers: America's Newest Parent Traps," *The Washington Post*, "Outlook" section, January 30, 1994, C3.

[20] See Fred A. Baughman, Jr., "Capable of Learning, Yet Failed by Their Schools," *Issues and Views*, Winter 1994, p. 13.

[21] Hillel Schwartz, "I Cry, I'm Shy, I'll Die," *The Washington Post*, "Outlook," February 6, 1994, C4. See Thomas Szasz, *The Therapeutic State: Psychiatry in the Mirror of Current Events* (Buffalo, N.Y.: Prometheus Books, 1984) and *The Theology of Medicine: The Political-Philosophical Foundations of Medical Ethics* (New York: Harper Colophon Books, 1977).

[22] John R. Lott, Jr., "Why Is Education Publicly Provided? A Critical Survey," *Cato Journal*, Fall 1987, pp. 495–96.

[23] Lippmann wrote about this in *Public Opinion* (1921; London: Allen & Unwin, 1932). See Edward S. Herman and Noam Chomsky, *Manufacturing Consent: The Political Economy of the Mass Media* (New York: Pantheon, 1988).

[24] Richard Mitchell, *The Graves of Academe* (New York: Fireside/ Simon & Schuster, 1981), pp. 7–8.

[25] And in fact, it is. In Jennifer's former school, children memorize "math facts," that is, they do not need to know what it means to add two numbers. They learn to recognize the sound and sight. For example, they have no idea why 2+3 has the same answer as 3+2. In helping to teach math to my children, who are home-schooled, I have discovered that I must have been subjected to the "math fact" approach when I was in school.

[26] Murray N. Rothbard, *Education, Free and Compulsory: The Individual's Education* (Wichita, Kans.: Center for Independent Education, undated), p. 7.

[27] Jonathan Kozol, *Savage Inequalities: Children in America's Schools* (New York: Crown Publishers, 1991), p. 54.

[28] Ibid., p. 222.

[29] Ibid., p. 223. Interestingly, Kozol elsewhere in his book quotes a big-city teacher who says, "'It's all a game. Keep them in class for seven years and give them a diploma if they make it to eighth grade. They can't read, but give them the diploma. The parents don't know what's going on. They're satisfied.'

"When I ask him if the lack of money and resources is a problem in the school, he looks amused by this. 'Money would be helpful but it's not the major factor,' he replies. 'The parents are the problem.'" (p. 48.)

[30] Quoted in William F. Rickenbacker, ed., *The Twelve-Year Sentence* (LaSalle, Ill.: Open Court, 1974), pp. 38–39.

[31] Rothbard, p. 6.

[32] The educational system, of course, is by no means the only factor that has eroded the family.

3

Why There Are
Public Schools

*Let our pupil be taught that he does not belong to himself, but that he is
public property. Let him be taught to love his family, but let him be taught at
the same time that he must forsake and even forget them when the welfare of his
country requires it.*

—Benjamin Rush
signer of the Declaration of Independence

W hy were the public schools ever established? Did the private
sector fail to set up schools or set up too few of them? Were large
segments of society barred from obtaining education? Was the
education of poor quality? The answer to the last three questions is
no. The public schools were not established to make up for any
deficiency in people's ability to learn to read, write, do arithmetic,
and acquire knowledge of other subjects. The government schools
were set up for another purpose entirely.

As Jack High and Jerome Ellig have written, "Private education
was widely demanded in the late 18th and 19th centuries in Great
Britain and America. The private supply of education was highly
responsive to that demand, with the consequence that large numbers
of children from all classes of society received several years of
education."[1]

High and Ellig show that the government's involvement in
education "displaced private education, sometimes deliberately
stifling it [and] altered the kind of education that was offered, mainly
to the detriment of the poorer working classes."[2] In colonial times

37

through the early Republic period, when private schools were the rule, a great many people were educated, despite the relatively low living standards of the day. As the historian Robert Seybolt wrote:

> In the hands of private schoolmasters the curriculum expanded rapidly. Their schools were commercial ventures, and, consequently, competition was keen. . . . Popular demands, and the element of competition, forced them not only to add new courses of instruction, but constantly to improve their methods and technique of instruction.[3]

Schooling in that early period was plentiful, innovative, and well within the reach of the common people. What effect did it have? High and Ellig note that 80 percent of New Yorkers leaving wills could sign their names. Other data show that from 1650 to 1795, male literacy climbed from 60 to 90 percent; female literacy went from 30 to 45 percent. Between 1800 and 1840, literacy in the North rose from 75 percent to between 91 and 97 percent. And in the South during the same span, the rate grew from 50–60 percent to 81 percent.[4] Indeed, Senator Edward M. Kennedy's office issued a paper not long ago stating that the literacy rate in Massachusetts has never been as high as it was before compulsory schooling was instituted. Before 1850, when Massachusetts became the first state in the United States to force children to go to school, literacy was at 98 percent. When Kennedy's office released the paper, it was 91 percent.[5]

According to Carl F. Kaestle, "Literacy was quite general in the middle reaches of society and above. The best generalization possible is that New York, like other American towns of the Revolutionary period, had a high literacy rate relative to other places in the world, and that literacy did not depend primarily upon the schools."[6] Another indication of the high rate of literacy is book sales. Thomas Paine's pamphlet *Common Sense* sold 120,000 copies in a colonial population of 3 million (counting the 20 percent who were slaves)—the equivalent of 10 million copies today. In 1818, when the United States had a population of under 20 million, Noah Webster's *Spelling Book* sold over 5 million copies. Walter Scott's novels sold that many copies between 1813 and 1823, which would be the equivalent of selling 60 million copies in the United States today. *The Last of the Mohicans* by James Fenimore Cooper sold millions of copies. John Taylor Gatto notes that Scott's and Cooper's books were not easy reading. European visitors to early nineteenth-century America—

such as Alexis de Tocqueville and Pierre du Pont de Nemours—marveled at how well educated the people were.[7]

High and Ellig sum up the experience of the 18th and 19th centuries by noting that "the available evidence strongly indicates that Americans of the period took an active interest in education. . . . The private supply was extensive, not only in the number of children served but in the spectrum of social classes involved."[8]

Thus, the rise of public, or government, schools was not a response to any inability on the part of society to provide for the education of its children. As Joel Spring has written, "The primary result of common school reform in the middle of the nineteenth century was not the education of increasing percentages of children, but the creation of new forms of school organization."[9] It should be obvious that the school systems were not set up merely to serve the poor. As Milton Friedman has noted, if the only motive were to help people who could not afford education, advocates of government involvement would have simply proposed tuition subsidies. After all, when proponents of government activism wanted to use the state to subsidize the purchase of food, they did not propose that government build a system of state grocery stores. They instead created food stamps. So the question is: Why are there public schools rather than "school stamps"?

School as propagandist

We may break down the reasons into two broad categories, the macro and the micro. The aim of the public schools at the macro, or social, level was the creation of a homogeneous, national, Protestant culture: the Americanization and Protestantization of the disparate groups that made up the United States. At the micro, or individual, level the aim was the creation of the Good Citizen, someone who trusted and deferred to government in all areas it claimed as its own. Obviously, the two levels are linked, because a certain culture cannot be brought about without remaking the individuals who comprise it.

Throughout history, rulers and court intellectuals have aspired to use the educational system to shape their nations. The model was set out by Plato in *The Republic* and was constructed most faithfully in Soviet Russia, Fascist Italy, and Nazi Germany. But one need not look only to extreme cases to find such uses of the educational system. One can see how irresistible a vehicle the schools would be to any social engineer. They represent a unique opportunity to mold future citizens early in life, to instill in them the proper reverence for the ruling culture, and to prepare them to be obedient and obeisant taxpayers and soldiers. Unsurprisingly, rulers and intellectuals jumped at the chance to make the schools a mill for the creation of Good Citizens. That motivation has been part of every effort to establish government schools.

The indispensable key to using the educational system for that purpose is compulsory attendance. Were children free to attend nonstate schools or to avoid formal schooling altogether, the state's effort would be thwarted. The state's apparently benevolent goal of universal education has actually been an insidious effort to capture all children in its net.

Union of school and state

Before looking at the American experience with compulsory public education, let's go back to the very origins of the link between school and state. One of the earliest, if not the first, full-blown state educational system was built in Sparta. "In Sparta, an ancient model for modern totalitarianism, the state was organized as one vast military camp, and the children were seized by the state and educated in barracks to the ideal of state obedience. Sparta early realized the logical, inevitable end result of a compulsory education system."[10] (The Spartan model was observed by Plato.)

The modern link between state and school was forged during the Protestant Reformation, before which education was in the hands of the church and various private educators. An early elaboration of the potential role of public schools was written by Martin Luther in his 1524 letter to the German authorities. Luther wrote:

> I maintain that the civil authorities are under obligation to compel the people to send their children to school. . . . If the government can compel such citizens as are fit for military service to bear the spear and rifle, to mount ramparts, and perform other material duties in time of war, how much more has it a right to compel the people to send their children to school, because in this case we are warring with the devil, whose object it is secretly to exhaust our cities and principalities of their strong men.[11]

The first modern public schools were founded in the German state of Gotha in 1524; three years later, Thuringa set up public schools. In 1559, compulsory attendance was inaugurated in Württemberg. Luther himself drew up a plan for Saxony. The purpose of all those school systems was to impose Lutheranism. Similarly, in the mid 16th century, John Calvin set up mandatory schools in Geneva, which were used to stamp out dissent. Under Calvin's influence, Holland followed suit in the beginning of the 17th century. It is important to understand that the purpose of the schools was to indoctrinate the citizens in the official religious outlook, for, as Luther put it, "no secular prince can permit his subjects to be divided by the preaching of opposite doctrines. . . . Heretics are not to be disputed with, but to be condemned unheard." Unsurprisingly, it was in Calvinist New England that compulsory schooling first arrived in America.

Europe's first national system of education was set up by King Frederick William I of Prussia in 1717. His son, Frederick the Great, following in his father's footsteps, said, "The prince is to the nation he governs what the head is to the man; it is his duty to see, think and act for the whole community." After the defeat at the hands of Napoleon in 1807, King Frederick William III strengthened the state's hold on society by, among other measures, increasing the power of the school system. He instituted certification of teachers and abolished semi-religious private schools. High-school graduation examinations were necessary to enter the learned professions and the civil service. Children aged 7 to 14 had to attend school. Parents could be fined or have their children taken away if the children did not attend. Private schools could exist only as long as they kept to the standards of the government's schools. An official language was imposed through the schools, to the prejudice of ethnic groups living in Prussia.[12]

When Germany emerged as a unified nation, the Prussian school system was enlarged. As Franz de Hovre wrote in 1917:

> The prime fundamental of German education is that it is based on a national principle. . . . A fundamental feature of German education: education to the State, education for the State, education by the State. The Volksschule is a direct result of a national principle aimed at national unity. The State is the supreme end in view.[13]

In 1910 Ernst Troeltsch pointed out the obvious: "The school organization parallels that of the army, the public school corresponds to the popular army." The German philosopher Johann Fichte was a key contributor to the formation of the German school system. It was Fichte who said that the schools "must fashion the person, and fashion him in such a way that he simply cannot will otherwise than what you wish him to will."

41

Importantly, American advocates of compulsory state schooling observed the Prussian system, became enamored of it, and
adopted it as their model. As former teacher John Taylor Gatto writes:

> A small number of very passionate American ideological lead-
> ers visited Prussia in the first half of the 19th century; fell in love
> with the order, obedience, and efficiency of its education
> system; and campaigned relentlessly thereafter to bring the
> Prussian vision to these shores. Prussia's ultimate goal was to
> unify Germany; the Americans' was to mold hordes of immi-
> grant Catholics to a national consensus based on a northern
> European cultural model. To do that, children would have to be
> removed from their parents and from inappropriate cultural
> influences.[14]

Gatto emphasizes how the Prussian model set the standard for
educational systems right up to the present. "The whole system was
built on the premise that isolation from first-hand information and
fragmentation of the abstract information presented by teachers
would result in obedient and subordinate graduates, properly re-
spectful of arbitrary orders," he writes. He says the American educa-
tionists imported three major ideas from Prussia. The first was that
the purpose of state schooling was not intellectual training but the
conditioning of children "to obedience, subordination, and collective life." Thus, memorization outranked thinking. Second, whole
ideas were broken into fragmented "subjects" and school days were
divided into fixed periods "so that self-motivation to learn would be
muted by ceaseless interruptions." Third, the state was posited as the
true parent of children. All of this was done in the name of a scientific
approach to education, although, Gatto says, "no body of theory
exists to accurately define the way children learn, or what learning
is of most worth."

To appreciate the nature of the Prussian system, let us look at
one of its innovations: kindergarten. In 1840, Friedrich Froebel
opened the first kindergarten, in Germany, as a way of socializing
children. "As the name implies," Spring writes, "the kindergarten
was conceived as a garden of children to be cultivated in the same
manner as plants."[15] Educators in America observed what was
happening in Germany and transplanted kindergarten to the New
World. In 1873, the first public school kindergarten was opened in
the United States, in St. Louis. Its purpose, according to school
superintendent William Torrey Harris, was to rescue children from
poverty and bad families by bringing them into the school system

early in life. "The child who passes his years in the misery of the crowded tenement house or alley becomes early familiar with all manner of corruption and immorality," Harris said. The kindergarten curriculum, writes Spring, included the teaching of moral habits, cleanliness, politeness, obedience, and self-control. The education historian Marvin Lazerson, in his study of the Boston school system, found that the administrators saw kindergarten as an indirect means of teaching slum parents how to run good homes. That represented a change from an earlier conception of kindergarten with its emphasis on play and expression. In the 20th century, the emphasis switched again, from reforming parents to reforming children and protecting them from their urban surroundings. The use of the school as a buffer between the child and his family and community led to the establishment of playgrounds and parks, and then summer schools— all intended to extend the school's influence over the child. The objective was to keep children busy. As a superintendent of schools in Massachusetts said in 1897, "The value of these [summer] schools consists not so much in what shall be learned during the few weeks they are in session, as in the fact that no boy or girl shall be left with unoccupied time. Idleness is an opportunity for evil-doing." Idleness apparently meant any time spent out of school. Joel Spring comments:

> By the early twentieth century the school in fact had expanded its functions into areas not dreamed of in the early part of the previous century. Kindergartens, playgrounds, school showers, nurses, social centers, and Americanization programs turned the school into a central social agency in urban America. The one theme that ran through all these new school programs was the desire to maintain discipline and order in urban life. Within this framework, the school became a major agency for social control.[16]

Today's advocates of "early intervention" and year-round school seem to share that objective.

It cannot be overemphasized that American schools, which have changed only slightly since the 19th century, were modeled on the authoritarian Prussian schools—not much of a recommendation. Albert Einstein was a product of those schools. Considering Einstein's intellectual achievements, that might suggest that the schools in Germany were of high quality. Before drawing that conclusion, however, hear Einstein's own words:

One had to cram all this stuff into one's mind, whether one liked it or not. This coercion had such a deterring effect that, after I had passed the final examination, I found the consideration of any scientific problems distasteful to me for an entire year. . . . It is in fact nothing short of a miracle that the modern methods of instruction have not yet entirely strangled the holy curiosity of inquiry; for this delicate little plant, aside from stimulation, stands mainly in need of freedom; without this it goes to wrack and ruin without fail. It is a very grave mistake to think that the enjoyment of seeing and searching can be promoted by means of coercion and a sense of duty. To the contrary, I believe that it would be possible to rob even a healthy beast of prey of its voraciousness, if it were possible, with the aid of a whip, to force the beast to devour continuously, even when not hungry—especially if the food, handed out under such coercion, were to be selected accordingly.[17]

Public schooling in America[18]

As noted, the first compulsory schools were in the colonies of New England (excluding Rhode Island). Five years before setting up public schools in 1647, Massachusetts Bay Colony passed a compulsory literacy law, which stated:

For as much as the good education of children is of singular behoof and benefit to any commonwealth, and whereas many parents and masters are too indulgent and negligent of their duty of that kind, it is ordered that the selectmen of every town . . . shall have a vigilant eye over their neighbors, to see first that none of them shall suffer so much barbarism in any of their families, as not to endeavor to teach, by themselves or others, their children and apprentices.

After the American Revolution, Massachusetts again spearheaded the compulsory-education movement. In 1852, the state set up the first modern government schooling system. It was not always smooth going for the enforcers, however. Some 80 percent of the people of Massachusetts resisted the imposition of public schooling. In 1880, it took the militia to persuade the parents of Barnstable, on Cape Cod, to give up their children to the system.[19] By 1900, nearly every state had government schools and compulsory attendance. At first, only elementary education was provided by the state. Later, the government system was extended to high school. These days, the many advocates of public schooling want the state to provide day care beginning at an early age and year-round schooling. The trend is unmistakable.

Because of the libertarian overtone of the American founding, it is not widely appreciated that some key figures in the Revolutionary period seemed more suited to Prussia than to the fledgling United States. A good example of that is Benjamin Rush, a physician and signer of the Declaration of Independence. He was also an early proponent of state control of education.[20] In 1786, Rush devised a plan for public schools in Pennsylvania. He wrote:

> It is necessary to impose upon them [children] the doctrines and discipline of a particular church. Man is naturally an ungovernable animal, and observations on particular societies and countries will teach us that when we add the restraints of ecclesiastical to those of domestic and civil government, we produce in him the highest degrees of order and virtue.[21]

Rush saw the schools as the means to "convert men into republican machines. This must be done if we expect them to perform their parts properly in the great machine of the government of the state." He also saw the schools as essential for making up for the failings of the deteriorating family. As he put it, "Society owes a great deal of its order and happiness to the deficiencies of parental government being supplied by those habits of obedience and subordination which are contracted at schools." He was clear about the role of schools. "The authority of our masters [should] be as absolute as possible," he said. "By this mode of education, we prepare our youth for the subordination of laws and thereby qualify them for becoming good citizens of the republic." He took that position because he believed that useful citizens were manufactured from children who "have never known or felt their own wills till they were one and twenty years of age."

One could quote Rush for many pages, each passage more horrifying than the last. Two more examples should suffice. What should the state schools teach the student? "He must be taught to amass wealth, but it must be only to increase his power of contribution to the wants and needs of the state." Furthermore, this signer of the Declaration said, "Let our pupil be taught that he does not belong to himself, but that he is public property. Let him be taught to love his family, but let him be taught at the same time that he must forsake and even forget them when the welfare of his country requires it."

The themes of obedience and the deficiencies of the family pervade the thinking of the early proponents of public schools. In 1816 Archibald D. Murphey, founder of the North Carolina public schools, wrote:

> In these schools the precepts of morality and religion should be inculcated, and habits of subordination and obedience be formed.... Their parents know not how to instruct them.... The state, in the warmth of her affection and solicitude for their welfare, must take charge of those children and place them in school where their minds can be enlightened and their hearts trained to virtue.[22]

Robert Dale Owen, founder of the experimental collective in New Harmony, Indiana, in the early 19th century, made clear yet again that the purpose of public education was not benefit of the child. "It is national, rational, republican education . . . for the honour, the happiness, the virtue, the salvation of the state."[23] Calvin Stowe, a 19th-century American educationist, sounded much like Luther when he said:

> If a regard to the public safety makes it right for a government to compel the citizens to do military duty when the country is invaded, the same reason authorizes the government to compel them to provide for the education of their children—for no foes are so much to be dreaded as ignorance and vice. A man has no more right to endanger the state by throwing upon it a family of ignorant and vicious children than he has to give admission to the spies of an invading army. If he is unable to educate his children, the state should assist him—if unwilling, it should compel him.[24]

The "schoolmaster of America," writes school historian Joel Spring, was Noah Webster, the lexicographer and textbook author. A major theme of Webster's work was nationalism, and Spring points out that Webster thought the schools and textbooks should encourage patriotism, develop an American language, and foster a national spirit. He was a Massachusetts legislator between 1815 and 1819, where he worked to establish a state school fund. In a speech to the legislature, he spelled out the salvation he hoped for from a system of "common schools":

I should rejoice to see a system adopted that should lay a foundation for a permanent fund for public schools, and to have more pains taken to discipline our youth in early life to sound maxims of moral, political, and religious duties. I believe more than is commonly believed may be done in this way towards correcting the vices and disorders of society.

The fostering of the right political values could be accomplished by the schools, Webster believed, because "good republicans . . . are formed by a singular machinery in the body politic, which takes the child as soon as he can speak, checks his natural independence and passions, makes him subordinate to superior age, to the laws of the state, to town and parochial institutions." Webster's *New England Primer* contained the "Federal Catechism," a series of questions and answers about political principles that children were expected to memorize in order to learn the values of citizenship and devotion to country.

The next major figure in the push for government-sponsored education was Horace Mann, who in 1837 became the first secretary of the Massachusetts Board of Education. He is the father of the common-school movement, which according to Joel Spring worked for "the establishment and standardization of state systems of education designed to achieve specific public policies." The movement understood that standardization required state-level agencies that controlled local school boards. The biggest difference between the common school and what went before was the idea that the school would be controlled by government in order to have children from different social backgrounds taught a common body of knowledge. "The term *common school*," Spring writes, "came to have a specific meaning: a school that was attended in common by all children and where a common political and social ideology was taught."[25] Historians have offered conflicting interpretations of the common-school and compulsory-education movement. Some see it intended as a cure for poverty, crime, and class tensions; others see it as a pro-democracy movement; others believe it was an upper-class movement motivated by a fear of instability in the working class; another group of writers sees it as a vast mill to serve the industrial system; and still others see it as a mechanism for imposing an American Protestant ideology. Barry Poulson points out that labor unions supported compulsory attendance laws because they kept children out of the workforce and reduced competition.[26] It is likely that all these intentions were at work in the movement. The key point is that each shared the view that the coercive apparatus of government should be used to override the preferences of free citizens and to interfere with the spontaneous growth of society; in other words, all were contrary to the liberalism on which the United States was founded. To the extent that the common-school founders saw the system as essential for the moral education of children, they were operating on an anti-family premise. Parents could not be trusted to raise children of high character. Once again, the government was thought to know better than parents in matters of morality, an area of life well within the grasp of common people. In an essential respect, then, the common school took children from their parents. As Horace Mann put it, "We who are engaged in the sacred cause of education are entitled to look upon all parents as having given hostages to our cause."

Mann had a fascinating set of interests. A former Calvinist, he became a devotee of phrenology (the "scientific" study of bumps on people's heads), temperance (out of a belief that alcohol prohibition would end crime and poverty), and the common school. It is no coincidence that Mann was interested in both phrenology and education; it was widely believed in his time that the skull's protuberances revealed character and mental ability. Mann is credited with basing his educational philosophy on science. It should be borne in mind that the "science" he based that philosophy on was *phrenology.*[27]

Mann indicated his belief in the redemptive potential of state education (and his role in it) when he was told he would be nominated to head the state board of education. In his journal he wrote, "what a diffusion, what intensity, what perpetuity of blessings he [the holder of that office] would confer! How would his beneficial influence upon mankind widen and deepen as it descended forever!" When he decided to accept the position, he wrote, "Henceforth, so long as I hold this office, I devote myself to the supremest welfare of mankind upon the earth. . . . I have faith in the improvability of the race." And in a letter to a friend, he explained that he was giving up the practice of law to take up education. "Having found the present generation composed of materials almost unmalleable, I am about transferring my efforts to the next. Men are cast-iron; but *children are wax.* Strength expended upon the latter may be effectual, which would make no impression upon the former." [Emphasis added.] Here again, we see a virtual denial that young human beings are autonomous beings with rights. Rather, they are seen as something to be shaped out of external considerations.

Because Mann wished the common school to provide a moral and political education for all children in order to end crime and corruption, he concluded that there should be no denominational religious teaching in the curriculum. Sectarianism would alienate parts of the community and destroy the mission of the common school. Yet, since in Mann's day moral teaching divorced from religion was unthinkable, he decided that using the Bible as a moral text would, in fact, be nondenominational and hence would not create tension among various religious groups.[28] He similarly feared that if divergent political ideas were taught in school "the tempest of political strife would be let loose." His solution was to admit into the common school only those ideas held by "all sensible and judicious men, all patriots, and all genuine republicans." Teachers were to avoid political disputes in the classroom. Again, in order to diminish social, political, and class conflict, he wished to steer clear of differences that would divide the community. Of course, those areas of political thought that had broad agreement were not likely to threaten the ruling political interests. The education establishment would soon see public education as the vehicle for "Americanizing" the wave of immigrants, particularly Catholics, from Europe.

Not all of Mann's goals were objectionable. For example, he believed that the common school would give all levels of society the means to earn wealth. Education, of course, can increase the opportunity to make money. But Mann seems to have other things in mind, as indicated by his belief that "education, then, beyond all other devices of human origin, is the great equalizer of the conditions of men—the balance-wheel of the social machinery." As discussed in the last chapter, the varied conditions of individuals are beyond anyone's power to "equalize." For Mann, equalization and social harmony would be advanced by the compulsory mixing of children from rich and poor families. Thus, the ideas of such modern-day egalitarians as Mickey Kaus are revealed as not so modern after all.[29]

Mann was by no means the only public school advocate who uttered presumptuous ideas about children. At the end of the 19th century, Edward Ross, a sociologist, argued that with the (alleged) erosion of the influence of religion, community, and family, the state needed other ways to exercise control over its citizens, especially the young, in the industrial age. "The ebb of religion," he said, "is only half a fact. The other half is the high tide of education. While the priest is leaving the civil service, the schoolmaster is coming in. As the state shakes itself loose from the church, it reaches out for the school." Ross perfectly illustrates the elitist thinker who scorns parents for being inferior guides for children. "Copy the child will, and the advantage of giving him his teacher instead of his father to imitate, is that the former is a picked person, while the latter is not." Ross eagerly saw the school as the means for gathering "little plastic lumps of human dough from private households and[shaping] them on the social kneadingboard."[30] Children as human dough on the social kneadingboard! An apt image for what Ross and Mann had in mind.

That image is similar to that held by the founders of the Progressive education movement and their inspiration, the pragmatist philosopher John Dewey. As a pragmatist, Dewey believed that there were no fixed principles that transcended social contexts and that therefore one should adopt ideas and values that "work" in the situation at hand. His politics were collectivist, and that was reflected in his approach to education, which he saw as fundamental to social reform. As Dewey wrote, "A society is a number of people held together because they are working along common lines, in a common spirit, and with references to common ends."[31] That, of course, was not the notion of society distinctive to America's revolutionary heritage; the American idea of society entailed a group of people who as individuals freely chose and pursued their own ends within a rule of law. Joel Spring points out that Dewey was one of the thinkers who provided the theoretical framework for the shift in education from individual to group work. As he wrote, "I believe that . . . education is a regulation of the process of coming to share in the social consciousness; and that the adjustment of individual activity on the basis of this social consciousness is the only sure method of social reconstruction." The school was to be anointed to prepare children for progressive society, which for Dewey meant a group orientation rather than an emphasis on the individual's intellectual development. He also wrote, "The social organism through the school, as its organ, may determine ethical results. . . . Through education society can formulate its own purposes, can organize its own means and resources, and thus shape itself with definiteness and economy in the direction in which it wishes to move."[32]

Dewey's views converged to create a bias against abstract learning and individualism. "The mere absorbing of facts and truths is so exclusively individual an affair that it tends very naturally to pass into selfishness. There is no obvious social motive for the acquirement of *mere learning,* there is no clear social gain in success thereat." [Emphasis added.][33] For the pragmatists, individual liberty, free economic competition, and limited government were obsolete and inappropriate principles in the prevailing social conditions. Unfortunately, most people, particularly parents, did not understand that truth. The schools would have to play the major role in preparing future citizens for the new society. For Dewey, the mission was sacred: "The teacher always is the prophet of the true God and the usherer-in of the true Kingdom of God."[34]

Educators today do not talk about schools and children the way they used to. It is not, I believe, because they think differently. Rather they are well schooled in a discipline that did not exist in Benjamin Rush's and Horace Mann's day: public relations. But every once in a while an educator forgets himself or does not realize that the rest of us are listening. William H. Seawell, professor of education at the University of Virginia, got caught in that position in 1981. He said, "Public schools promote civic rather than individual pursuits" and, "We must focus on creating citizens for the good of society."[35] But most startlingly, he said, "Each child belongs to the state." There was no outcry from the public. Of course, the coercive power of government lies behind all such utterances. That was made clear in South Africa, during its first all-race election. Campaigning in a poor area of the country, Winnie Mandela promised "free and compulsory education" to all, adding to loud applause (!), "Parents not sending their children to school will be the first prisoners of the ANC [African National Congress] government."[36]

Despite their differences, the thinkers discussed in this chapter shared at least one principle: they believed that the school should be the mechanism through which the state, run by the intellectual elite, would shape the youth of the nation. In a word, the schools' business would be indoctrination.

In summary, the public schools have from the beginning been antagonists of liberty and the spontaneous order of liberal market society. In such an order, individuals choose their own ends and engage in peaceful means, competitive and cooperative, to achieve them. They also raise their children according to their own values and by their own judgment. In contrast, public schools have been intended to interfere with that free development and to mold youth into loyal, compliant servants of the state. Their objectives have required a rigidity and authoritarianism that is inconsistent with the needs of a growing rational being seeking knowledge about the world. Thus, the schools are a source of immense frustration for many children. It should surprise no one that those schools produce children who are passive, bored, aimless, and even worse: self-destructive and violent. The earliest critics of public schools would not have been surprised.

The founders of government-sponsored education were, until recently, rather candid about their objectives. From Sparta to Prussia to Massachusetts, the architects of public schooling believed they knew better than parents how to raise children. They presumed that the spontaneous growth of civil society was inferior to the social blueprints they had drawn up for their fellow citizens. In short, they were perfect examples of what Adam Smith, in *The Theory of Moral Sentiments,* called "the man of system," who

> seems to imagine that he can arrange the different members of a great society with as much ease as the hand arranges the different pieces upon a chess-board. He does not consider that the pieces upon a chess-board have no other principle of motion besides that which the hand impresses upon them; but that in the great chess-board of human society, every single piece has a principle of motion of its own, altogether different from that which the legislature might choose to impress upon it.

The men of system who imposed public schooling on the rest of society did not go unanswered. In the next chapter, we will examine what the opponents of state education had to say.

Notes

[1] Jack High and Jerome Ellig, "The Private Supply of Education: Some Historical Evidence," in Tyler Cowen, ed., *The Theory of Market Failure* (Fairfax, Va.: George Mason University Press/Cato Institute, 1988), pp. 378⁻79.

[2] Ibid., p. 362.

[3] Robert F. Seybolt, *Source Studies in American Colonial Education: The Private School* (1925; New York: Oxford University Press, 1971), p. 102.

[4] Barry W. Poulson, "Education and the Family During the Industrial Revolution," in Joseph R. Peden and Fred R. Glahe, eds., *The American Family and the State* (San Francisco: Pacific Research Institute, 1986), p. 138.

[5] See John Taylor Gatto, *Dumbing Us Down: The Hidden Curriculum of Compulsory Schooling* (Philadelphia: New Society Publishers, 1992), pp. 25⁻26.

[6] Carl F. Kaestle, *The Evolution of an Urban School System: New York City 1750–1850* (Cambridge, Mass.: Harvard University Press, 1973), p. 5.

[7] This paragraph is drawn from John Taylor Gatto, "Our Prussian School System," *Cato Policy Report*, March/April 1993.

[8] High and Ellig, p. 373.

[9] Joel Spring, *The American School, 1642–1885* (New York: Longman, 1986), p. 112.

[10] Murray N. Rothbard, *Education, Free and Compulsory: The Individual's Education* (Wichita, Kans.: Center for Independent Education, undated), p. 18.

[11] Quoted in Murray N. Rothbard, "Historical Origins," in William F. Rickenbacker, ed., *The Twelve-Year Sentence* (LaSalle, Ill.: Open Court, 1974), p. 12.

[12] *Education, Free and Compulsory*, p. 25.

[13] Quoted from *German and English Education, a Comparative Study* in ibid., p. 27.

[14] Gatto, "Our Prussian School System," p. 10; subsequent quotations from Gatto are from the same article. Gatto is the former New York State and City Teacher of the Year who in his acceptance address denounced the schools as antichild and antifamily. See *Dumbing Us Down* and *The Exhausted School* (New York: Oxford Village Press, 1993).

¹⁵ Spring, p. 160.

¹⁶ Ibid., pp. 168–69.

¹⁷ Quoted in Paul Goodman, *Compulsory Mis-education* and *The Community of Scholars* (New York: Vintage Books, 1964), p. 6.

¹⁸ As this book was being completed, an intriguing new book came to my attention: Loraine Smith Pangle and Thomas L. Pangle, *The Learning of Liberty: The Educational Ideas of the American Founders* (Lawrence, Kans.: University Press of Kansas, 1993).

¹⁹ Gatto, *Dumbing Us Down*, p. 25.

²⁰ Rush was also the father of American psychiatry. Among his "discoveries" was that blacks actually suffered a form of leprosy. See Thomas S. Szasz, *The Manufacture of Madness* (New York: Delta, 1970), pp. 137–59. He also believed that lying was a "corporeal disease." Szasz writes that "Rush makes us realize how unoriginal, but yet how enduring, are the therapeutic posturings of the modern psychiatrist" (p. 157).

²¹ Quoted in Spring, pp. 33–34. Unless otherwise stated, the quotes from Rush and other school advocates are from Spring's book.

²² Quoted in *Education, Free and Compulsory*, p. 45.

²³ Quoted in ibid., p. 46.

²⁴ Quoted in ibid., pp. 50–51. Stowe's book was titled *The Prussian System of Public Instruction and Its Applicability to the United States.*

²⁵ Spring, p. 71.

²⁶ Poulson, p. 144.

²⁷ As the philosopher Bruce Goldberg points out in a forthcoming book, the scientific bases of later educational approaches have been no better than Mann's.

²⁸ Ironically, in New York in the 1840s, a conflict erupted between Catholics and Protestants over the public schools. The Catholics had their own school system, having been alienated from the public schools by their use of the King James Version of the Bible and textbooks that used the disparaging term "Popery" and referred to "deceitful Catholics." The Catholics petitioned for money from the common-school fund and complained of having to support the public schools and pay for their own schools. Feelings were so heated that there were riots in 1842. The state legislature sought a compromise by allowing local school boards to have more authority, but the

Catholics were not satisfied. A similar conflict occurred in Philadelphia. See Spring, pp. 101–107.

[29] See Mickey Kaus, *The End of Equality* (New York: New Republic Books, 1992), wherein he writes, "The upper middle class, with its impulses toward self-segregation, will have to be bought off or *beaten down.* . . . A big part of the problem is that the suburbs are autonomous jurisdictions, and we're trying to get them to do something they might democratically not want to do." (pp. 153–54, emphasis added).

[30] Quoted in Spring, p. 155. For the record, Thomas Jefferson also advocated state-sponsored schools. But he did not see them as molders of children's character. Rather, he merely wanted the schools to teach reading, writing, and arithmetic for three years. But, as Spring has pointed out, even Jefferson could not "resist the temptation of using the educational system to perpetuate what he considered to be political truth." Nevertheless, Jefferson opposed compulsory attendance; he said, "It is better to tolerate the rare instance of a parent refusing to let his child be educated than to shock the common feelings and ideas by the forcible asportation [carrying away] and education of the infant against the will of the father." (Rothbard, *Education, Free and Compulsory*, p. 42.)

[31] From John Dewey, *The School and Society*; quoted in Spring, p. 174.

[32] The remaning quotations in this paragraph come from *John Dewey on Education: Selected Writings*, ed. Reginald D. Archambault, quoted in Arthur J. Newman, ed., *In Defense of American Public Schools* (Cambridge, Mass.: Schenkman Publishing Co., 1978), pp. 23–24.

[33] From John Dewey, *The School and Society*; quoted in Ayn Rand, "The Comprachicos," in her *The New Left: The Anti-Industrial Revolution* (New York: New American Library, 1971), p. 172.

[34] *John Dewey on Education,* quoted in Newman, p. 24.

[35] Quoted in Richard Mitchell, *The Leaning Tower of Babel* (New York: Fireside/Simon & Schuster, 1984), pp. 272–73.

[36] Francis Mdlongwa, "Mandela's Wife Gives Voters Radical Gospel," (Reuter News Agency) *The Washington Times*, April 28, 1994.

4

Opponents of Public Schools

Men had better be without education than be educated by their rulers.
—Thomas Hodgskin

A few heroic voices spoke out against the public-school movement. They were radical and articulate voices. They objected to the authoritarianism inherent in government schools and abhorred the indoctrination and subordination that masqueraded as teaching. But their criticisms did not carry the day.

In England, those critics were called Voluntaryists, whose movement was a result of the tradition of independent education that grew out of the repression of Dissenters and Nonconformists after the Restoration of Charles II in 1660.[1] America too had its trenchant critics of public schools. Josiah Warren said in 1833 that federal aid to education would be like "paying the fox to take care of the chickens." Gerrit Smith, a radical abolitionist, put the case simply: "It is justice and not charity which the people need at the hands of government. Let government restore to them their land, and what other rights they have been robbed of, and they will then be able to pay for themselves—to pay their schoolmasters, as well as their parsons." Other advocates of the separation of state and school were William Youmans, editor of *The Popular Science Monthly*, and John Bonham, both admirers of English individualist Herbert Spencer.

In England, Joseph Priestly, the chemist and Dissenting minister, was the first prominent opponent of public schools. (See his *Essay on the First Principles of Government*.) Another early critic was William Godwin, who wrote in his *Enquiry Concerning Political Justice* (1793), "Government will not fail to employ it [education], to strengthen its hands, and perpetuate its institutions." Unfortunately, as libertarian historian Smith writes, by the 1860s the Voluntaryist movement had been co-opted by the stampeding movement for state education in England. When the Voluntaryists decided that state education was unstoppable, they switched sides in an attempt to shape the new system in acceptable ways. Some even accepted compulsory attendance. (The radical individualists Herbert Spencer and Auberon Herbert were not among those who made these fatal compromises.)

Wilhelm von Humboldt

An important critic of national education outside of England was Wilhelm von Humboldt, the German liberal and author of the influential book *The Limits of State Action*, written in 1792.[2] Humboldt's "grand, leading principle," as he put it, was "the absolute and essential importance of human development in its richest diversity." He was concerned that a system of national education would interfere with that development and enervate the people. As he put it, "National education, since at least it presupposes selection and appointment of some particular instructor, must always promote a definite form of development, however careful to avoid such an error." The state values tranquility above all else, he said, and will educate its subjects so as to "produce and maintain" that tranquility. The result is "sterility or lack of energy" in the individual who is subjected to that education. In contrast, private schools are interested in the person and will educate him "more surely without sacrifice of energy, through a variety of relationships."

Humboldt went on to argue that the national schools could not be confined simply to the task of encouraging spontaneous development, for "whatever has unity of organization invariably produces a corresponding uniformity of results, and thus, even when based on such principles, the utility of national education is still inconceivable." Besides, Humboldt added:

> If education is only to develop a man's faculties, without regard to giving human nature any special civil character, there is no need for the State's interference. Among men who are really free, every form of industry becomes more rapidly improved— all the arts flourish more gracefully—all the sciences extend their range. In such a community, too, family ties become closer; parents are more eagerly devoted to the care of their children, and, in a state of greater well-being, are better able to carry out their wishes with regard to them. . . . There would,

therefore, be no want of careful family training, nor of those private educational establishments which are so useful and indispensable.

He also argued that the state cannot be an effective moral teacher. "However great the influence of education may be, and however it may extend to the whole course of a man's actions, still, the circumstances which surround him throughout his whole life are far more important." Thus, for these reasons, Humboldt concluded that "national education seems to me to lie wholly beyond the limits within which the State's activity should properly be confined."

Herbert Spencer

Among the most systematic critics of state education was the great libertarian Herbert Spencer. In his first book, *Social Statics*,[3] Spencer devoted a chapter to the rights of children, proclaiming that his Law of Equal Freedom—every man has freedom to do all that he wills, provided he infringes not the equal freedom of any other man— "applies as much to the young as to the mature." He opposed coercive education, moral and otherwise, because, like other violations of Spencer's Law, it brought bad consequences. As he put it:

> Contrasting the means to be employed [namely, coercion] with the work to be done [character formation], we are at once struck with their utter unfitness. Instead of creating a new internal state which shall exhibit itself in better deeds, coercion can manifestly do nothing but forcibly mold externals into a coarse semblance of such a state. In the family, as in society, it can simply restrain; it cannot educate. . . . As someone has well said, the utmost that severity can do is make hypocrites; it can never make converts.

Spencer also objected to the coercive financing of education. In his view, government may act only to maintain rights, but that objective is no part of national education. He argued that the parent's failure to educate his child does not violate the child's rights. Note that he draws a sharp distinction between legality and morality; his concern here is solely with the legitimacy of coercion. "Omitting instruction in no way takes from the child's freedom to do whatsoever it wills in the best way it can, and this freedom is all that equity demands. . . . Consequently, however wrong the non-performing of a parental duty may be, however much it is condemned by the secondary morality—the morality of beneficence—it does not amount to a breach of the law of equal freedom and cannot therefore be taken cognizance of by the state."

Spencer, moreover, argued that once the premise of public education is granted, there is no reason why government should not assume responsibility for other aspects of childrearing, clothing, food, shelter, and so on, thereby "annulling all parental responsibility altogether." (Indeed, this is advocated by some people for inner-city children today.) He also pointed out that if the government declares a right to education, it must define education, opening the floodgates to a multitude of evils.

> For what is an education? Where, between the teaching of a dame-school and the most comprehensive university *curriculum*, can be drawn the line separating that portion of mental culture which may be justly claimed of the state from that which may not be so claimed? . . . When those who demand a state education can say exactly how much is due—can agree upon what the young have a right to, and what not—it will be time to listen. But until they accomplish this impossibility, their plea cannot be entertained.

Next, Spencer pointed out that if government ought to educate people, it is government that must determine the purpose and methods of education.

> Hence the proposition is convertible into this—a government ought to mold children into good citizens, using its own discretion in settling what a good citizen is and how the child may be molded into one. . . . Being thus justified in carrying out rigidly such plans as it thinks best, every government ought to do what the despotic governments of the Continent and of China do.

Spencer said the serious advocate of state education should wish to see private schools outlawed and books threatening to the government prohibited. "Now a minute dictation like this, which extends to every action and will brook no nay, is the legitimate realization of this state-education theory," he wrote.

Spencer further noted that people usually agree that parents love their children and go to great lengths to serve their interests. But all that is forgotten when attention turns to education.

It seems that this apparatus of feelings is wholly insufficient to work out the desideratum [of education], that this combination of affections and interests was not provided for such a purpose, or, what is the same thing, that it has no purpose at all. And so, in default of any natural provision for supplying the exigency, legislators exhibit to us the design and specification of a state machine, made up of masters, ushers, inspectors, and councils, to be worked by a due proportion to taxes, and to be plentifully supplied with raw material, in the shape of little boys and girls, out of which it is to grind a population of well-trained men and women who shall be "useful members of the community"!

Spencer then turned to the argument that parents don't know of what a good education consists. He quoted John Stuart Mill, who wrote, "In the matter of education, the [government's] intervention is justifiable; because the case is one in which the interest and judgment of the consumer are not sufficient security for the goodness of the commodity." Mill's position on education was muddled. In *On Liberty,* Mill also wrote that the government should make a minimum education compulsory and help the poor to pay for it. He also said that a government school system "should only exist, *if it exists at all,* as one among many competing experiments, carried on for the purpose of example and stimulus, to keep the others up to a certain standard of excellence [emphasis added]." Yet he warned that "a general State education is a mere contrivance for moulding people to be exactly like one another; and as the mould in which it casts them is that which pleases the predominant power of the government, whether this be a monarch, a priesthood, an aristocrat, or the majority of the existing generation in proportion as it is efficient and successful, it establishes a despotism over the mind, leading by natural tendency to one over the body."

With characteristic keenness, Spencer took Mill on in the matter of parents' not being qualified to judge education:

It is strange that so judicious a writer should feel satisfied with such a worn-out excuse. This alleged incompetency on the part of the people has been the reason assigned for all state interferences whatever. . . . A stock argument for the state teaching of religion has been that the masses cannot distinguish false religion from true. There is hardly a single department of life over which, for similar reasons, legislative supervision has not been, or may not be, established.

His reply to Mill and to those who share that view was that experience teaches that "in the long run, the interest of the consumer is not only an efficient guarantee for the goodness of the things consumed, but the best guarantee." He added:

> People are not, after all, such incompetent judges of education as they seem. Ignorant parents are generally quick enough to discern the effects of good or bad teaching; will note them in the children of others and act accordingly. Moreover, it is easy for them to follow the example of the better instructed and choose the same schools. Or they may get over the difficulty by asking advice. . . . Lastly, there is the test of price. With education, as with other things, price is a tolerably safe index of value, and it is open to all classes, and it is one which the poor instinctively appeal to in the matter of schools, for it is notorious that they look coldly at very cheap or gratuitous instruction.

Mill's statement assumes that the state is a better judge of education than the incompetent parents and will look out for their children's interests. Is that premise justified? asked Spencer. He answered by observing that the men of the governing class see things differently from other people. "Very comfortable lives are led by the majority of them, and hence 'things as they are' find favor in their eyes," he wrote. "Now could the judgment of such respecting the commodity—education—be safely relied on? Certainly not." What of the interests of the rulers? Using public-choice analysis well before it became a formal school of economics, he replied:

> The self-seeking which, consciously or unconsciously, sways rulers in other cases, would sway them in this likewise—could not fail to do so—while the character of men is what it is. . . . We may be quite sure that a state education would be administered for the advantage of those in power rather than for the advantage of the nation. To hope for anything else is to fall into the old error of looking for grapes from thorns. Nothing can be more truly Utopian than expecting that, with men and things as they are, the influences which have vitiated all other institutions would not vitiate this one.

Spencer extended that argument by noting how education is particularly ill-suited for government jurisdiction, because government organizations are always conservative, that is, resistant to change, which threatens them. On the other hand, he wrote:

62

Education, properly so called, is closely associated with change, is its pioneer, is the never-sleeping agent of revolution, is always fitting men for higher things and unfitting them for things as they are. Therefore, between institutions whose very existence depends upon man continuing what he is and true education, which is one of the instruments for making him something other than he is, there must always be enmity.

He followed that argument with historical examples from ancient Egypt, Athens, Rome, China, and England, where at Oxford the works of Newton and Locke were shut out for a time.

Spencer closed his chapter by arguing that the costs of education are not fully accounted for. What he had in mind was not monetary cost but the loss of character that compulsory state-supported education brings about. He noted that man's most necessary quality is self-restraint, which he defined as "the ability to sacrifice a small present gratification for a prospective great one." Next, he established that the ablest teacher of self-restraint is experience. As he put it, "The only cure for imprudence is the suffering which imprudence entails." Spencer thought in evolutionary terms, so he made the point in appropriate language:

Let us never forget that the law is adaption to circumstances, be they what they may. And if, rather than allow men to come in contact with the real circumstances of their position, we place them in artificial—in false—circumstances, they will adapt themselves to these instead; and will, in the end, have to undergo the miseries of a readaption to the real ones.

The strongest incentive to develop self-restraint, Spencer wrote, is the sense of parental responsibility. Thus, anything that reduces that sense prevents self-restraint from being developed. State schools make the education of children appear free. Government-provided education seems to relieve parents of the responsibility of having to pay for an important part of raising their children. Can that have no consequence? "The more the state undertakes to do for his family," he wrote, "the more are the expenses of the married man reduced, at the cost of the unmarried man, and the greater becomes the temptation to marry. Let us not think that the offer of apparently gratuitous instruction for his offspring would be of no weight with the working-man deliberating on the propriety of taking a wife."

But that is not all. The effects would endure even after the children were born. "Free" education assures that there is one less reason for parents to resist the ubiquitous temptation to think and live short-range. As Spencer put it:

> Many a man who, as things are, can but just keep the mastery over some vicious or extravagant propensity, and whose most efficient curb is the thought that if he gives way it must be at the sacrifice of that book learning which he is ambitious to give his family, would fall were this curb weakened—would not only cease to improve in power of self-control as he is now doing, but would probably retrograde and bequeath his offspring to a lower instead of a higher phase of civilization. Hence . . . a government can educate in one direction only by *un*educating in another—can confer knowledge only at the expense of character.

Times and sexual ethics have changed since Spencer's day. "Free" education may not encourage marriage any longer. It may merely be one more bit of encouragement to have children out of wedlock, for schooling becomes one less factor in the cost calculus. Thus, government education along with the rest of the welfare state has the effect not only of eroding families, but of preventing their formation in the first place. Some might object that the erosion of the family has occurred in the last thirty years, but the public schools have existed for more than a hundred years. That objection ignores the fact that a culture can ride on its momentum for some period. But it cannot do so forever. The friction of state paternalism eventually slows the culture in its course and causes it to reverse direction. As Charles Murray and others have pointed out, the dire consequences of the welfare state's subversion of the family—especially the growing number of fatherless boys—are all around us.

Auberon Herbert

A leading disciple of Spencer's, Auberon Herbert, found another form of dependence fostered by the public schools in his 1880 essay "State Education: A Help or Hindrance?"[4] Herbert stated as a maxim that "no man or class accepts the position of receiving favors without learning, in the end, that these favors become disadvantages." He then asserted that state education is a political favor: "Whenever one set of people pay for what they do not use themselves, but what is used by another set of people, their payment is and must be of the nature of a favor, and does and must create a sort of dependence," namely, the dependence of working people on the upper classes, whose members run the school systems. "The most striking result [of public education] is that the wealthier class think that it is their right and their duty to direct the education of the people. They deserve no blame. As long as they pay by rate and tax for a part of this education, they undoubtedly possess a corresponding right of direction." So "the workman is selling his birthright for the mess of pottage. Because he accepts the rate and tax paid by others, he must accept the intrusion of these others into his own home affairs—the management and education of his children."

The remedy for that dependence, Herbert wrote, was for the working class to renounce the school system, "reject all forced contributions from others, and do their own work through their own voluntary combinations." He expected that "the most healthy state of education will exist when the workmen, dividing themselves into natural groups according to their own tastes and feelings, organize the education of their children without help, or need of help, from outside."

Herbert understood that schools cannot be run well democratically. The issues are complex, making representation problematic. "A mixed mass of men, like a nation," he said, "can only administer by suppressing differences and disregarding conviction." But when an educational system suppresses differences, it is acting contrary to its purpose. Only voluntary organization can avoid that problem, Herbert thought.

He also addressed the question of national standards, which are all the rage today. First, he told his countrymen that they should not be deceived by the appearance of localism in the public schools. In a passage that sounds like a description of modern America, Herbert wrote that apparently local and independent school boards "must use the same class of teachers; they must submit to the same inspectors; the children must be prepared for the same examination, and pass in the same standards." The few differences are minor. But, wrote Herbert, citing Spencer, "progress is difference," and the eradication of differences is the banishment of progress. A government education bureaucracy is fatal to differences and thus progress. Herbert explained:

> If, for example, a man holding new views about education can at once address himself to those in sympathy with him, can at once collect funds and proceed to try his experiment, he sees his goal in front of him, and labors in the expectation of obtaining some practical result to his labor. But if some great official system blocks the way, if he has to overcome the stolid resistance of a department, to persuade a political party, which has

no sympathy with views holding out no promise of political advantage, to satisfy inspectors, whose eyes are trained to see perfection of only one kind, and who may summarily condemn his school as "inefficient," and therefore disallowed by law, if in the meantime he is obliged by rates and taxes to support a system to which he is opposed, it becomes unlikely that his energy and confidence in his own views will be sufficient to inspire a successful resistance to such obstacles.[5]

When Herbert anticipated an objection to his argument—that the bureaucracy will be responsive to public opinion—he resorted to what has become known as rational-ignorance analysis:

When a state department becomes charged with some great undertaking, there accumulates so much technical knowledge round its proceedings, that without much labor and favorable opportunities it becomes exceedingly difficult to criticize successfully its action. It is a serious study in itself to follow the minutes and the history of a great department, either like the Local Board or the Education Department. And if a discussion should arise, the same reason makes it difficult for the public to form a judgment in the matter. A great office which is attacked envelopes [sic] itself, like a cuttlefish, in a cloud of technical statements which successfully confuses the public, until its attention is drawn off in some other direction. It is for this reason, I think, that state departments escape so easily from all control, and that such astounding cases of recklessness and mismanagement come periodically to light, making a crash which startles everybody for the moment.

That was written in England in 1880. It sounds like it was written yesterday in the United States.

Bureaucracies, Herbert wrote, are rigid and fearful of setting in motion changes that threaten them; they are blunt instruments. He pointed out the dilemma of letting a bureaucracy run the educational system: either the bureaucrats are free to exercise discretion or they must act within strict guidelines aimed at particular results. Neither alternative is good. The problems of bureaucratic discretion are obvious. Yet a results-oriented system, which is popular today, "necessarily restricts and vulgarizes our conceptions of education. It reduces everybody concerned . . . to the one aim and object of satisfying certain regulations made for them, of considering success in passing standards and success in education as the same thing." It is particularly bad for the dedicated teacher, who is turned into a clerk. "In all cases he must subdue his strongest tastes and feelings, and recast and remodel himself until he is a sufficiently humble copy of the inspector or examiner, upon whose verdict his success depends. Any plan better fitted to reduce managers, teachers, and pupils to one level of commonplace and stupidity could scarcely be found."

The priority of liberty

As George Smith notes, the English critics of national education saw the issue as a conflict between liberty and power.[6] They chose liberty. They knew there was no conflict between liberty and education. But if there were such a conflict, they knew which side they were on. "Liberty is more precious than education," said the Voluntaryist Richard Hamilton. "We love education, but there are things which we love better." Edward Baines seconded the sentiment: liberty, he said, is essential to "all the virtues which dignify men and communities." Thomas Hodgskin put it somewhat differently: "Men had better be without education than be educated by their rulers." The Voluntaryists denounced all aspects of state education: compulsory attendance was "child-kidnapping"; state inspection of schools was "government surveillance." Baines described state education as "a vast intellectual policy, set to watch over the young at the most critical period of their existence, to prevent the intrusion of dangerous thoughts, and turn their minds into safe channels."

The Voluntaryists repeatedly pointed out that similarity between educational freedom and religious and other civil liberties. As Baines wrote:

> In my judgment, the State could not consistently assume the support and control of education, without assuming the support and control of both the *pulpit* and the *press*. Once decide that Government money and Government superintendence are essential in the schools, whether to ensure efficiency, or to guard against abuse, ignorance, and error, and the self-same reasons will force you to apply Government money and Government superintendence to our periodical literature and our religious instruction.

The advocates of government schools accused the Voluntaryists of defending bad schools, a charge heard to this day. Baines faced the issue head on:

In one sense I am [an advocate of bad schools]. I maintain that we have as much right to have wretched schools as to have wretched newspapers, wretched preachers, wretched books, wretched institutions, wretched political economists, wretched Members of Parliament, and wretched Ministers. You cannot proscribe all these things without proscribing Liberty. The man is a simpleton who says, that to advocate Liberty is to advocate badness. The man is a quack and *doctrinaire* of the worst German breed, who would attempt to force all minds, whether individual or national, into a mould of ideal perfection, to stretch it out or to lop it down to his own Procrustean standard. I maintain that Liberty is the chief cause of excellence; but it would cease to be Liberty if you proscribed everything inferior. Cultivate giants if you please; but do not stifle dwarfs.

The Voluntaryists were also fearful that government would use the educational system in a self-serving, propagandistic way. The Voluntaryist journal *The Eclectic Review* had this to say in 1843:

It is no trifling thing to commit to any hands the moulding of the minds of men. An immense power is thus communicated, the tendency of which will be in exact accordance with the spirit and policy of those who use it. Governments, it is well known, are conservative. The tendency of official life is notorious, and it is the height of folly, the mere vapouring of credulity, to imagine that the educational system, if entrusted to the minister of the day, will not be employed to diffuse amongst the rising generation, that spirit and those views which are most friendly to his policy. By having, virtually, at his command, the whole machinery of education, he will cover the land with a new class of officials, whose dependence on his patronage will render them the ready instruments of his pleasure.

The horde of state teachers, warned the *Review,* would constitute a patronage system, whose sympathies will be with those who pay their salaries. The journal condemned this "criminal attempt of short-sighted flagitious politicians, to mould the intellect of the people to their pleasure." The Voluntaryists spurned those, such as the Dissenters, who sought to have state involvement in education without control and indoctrination. As Algernon Wells put it, the question is not "How can we obtain Government money? But, How can we avoid it?" His warning sounds as if he were talking to modern advocates of school vouchers:

They [Dissenters] must hold themselves entirely clear of all temptations to ask, when their public testimony is required,—How will our conduct affect our grants? The belief of many Independents is that, from the hour they received Government money, they would be a changed people—their tone lowered—their spirit altered—their consistency sacrificed—and their honour tarnished.

Like Spencer and Herbert, other radical critics of state education worried about the quashing of creativity in a uniform government school system. Joseph Priestly said education is an art requiring "experiments and trials." The true purpose of education needs "unbounded liberty, and even caprice. . . ," he said. "From new, and seemingly irregular, methods of education, perhaps something extraordinary and uncommonly great may spring." He added that the "great excellence of human nature consists in the variety of which it is capable. Instead, then, of endeavoring, by uniform and fixed systems of education, to keep mankind always the same, let us give free scope to everything which may bid fair for introducing more variety among us."

The Voluntaryists admirably lacked what F. A. Hayek identified as the misapprehension of reason as being able to anticipate the future sufficiently to predetermine the finest details of institutions. They understood that a state educational system would essentially be frozen and adverse to the unplanned, unexpected development that individuals and voluntary organizations experience and need to flourish. As Wells put it:

> How to teach, how to improve children, are questions admitting of new and advanced solutions, no less than inquiries how best to cultivate the soil, or to perfect manufactures. And these improvements cannot fail to proceed indefinitely, so long as education is kept wide open, and free to competition, and to all those impulses which liberty constantly supplies. But once close up this great science and movement of mind from these invigorating breezes, whether by monopoly or bounty, whether by coercion or patronage, and the sure result will be torpor and stagnancy.

The Eclectic Review pointed out that if all children are to be taught in identical ways, the teachers will first have to be so taught. "All teachers will be imbued with the same spirit. And under their cold and lifeless tuition, the national spirit, now warm and independent,

69

will grow into a type formal and dull, one harsh outline with its crisp edges, a mere complex machine driven by external impulse, with its appendages of apparent power but of gross resistance."

Being advocates of unfettered capitalism, the Voluntaryists often compared the market for education with the market for any other service or product. To them, the argument for free trade in education was the same as that for a free market in material products. (They drew that comparison for their laissez-faire compatriots who inconsistently supported state education, like the great free-trader Richard Cobden.) Applying this economic approach, *The Eclectic Review* wondered how a government school system would affect private educational efforts:

> How will it affect the balance between supply and demand; disturb the relations of the voluntary teacher, and misdirect the expectations and confidence of the market? Let a private teacher attempt to come into competition with such accredited and endowed agents of an incorporate system . . . and he will find himself in the same state with a merchant who ventures to trade without a bounty in competition with those whose traffic is encouraged by large public bounties.

In other words, private schools would have trouble competing with public schools. Their market would be constricted because the state system would have access to tax revenues and would appear to charge less than the private schools.

The American critics

In America, among the most penetrating social analysts was H. L. Mencken, the journalist and self-styled libertarian whose influence dominated America in the 1910s and 1920s. As an advocate of liberty and individualism, he could not abide a system that sought to turn human diversity into a homogeneous mass. That, he knew, was the ultimate aim of public schools.

> [The popular] erroneous assumption is to the effect that the aim of public education is to fill the young of the species with knowledge and awaken their intelligence. And so make them fit to discharge the duties of citizenship in an enlightened and independent manner. Nothing could be further from the truth. The aim of public education is not to spread the enlightenment

at all; it is simply to reduce as many individuals as possible to the same safe level, to breed a standard citizenry, to put down dissent and originality.[7]

For that reason, wrote Mencken, "A healthy boy is in constant revolt against the sort of men who surround him at school. Their puerile pedantries, their Christian Endeavor respectability, their sedentary pallor, their curious preference for the dull and uninteresting . . . In every boy's school the favorite teacher is the one who occasionally swears like a cavalry man, or is reputed to keep a jug in his room, or is known to receive a scented note every morning."

To those who believe the public schools once worked, hear Mr. Mencken from 1934:

> There is a general feeling that something is wrong with the public schools. The tendency is to blame the schoolma'ams. They seem to be responsible for the fact that the children learn very little and are generally bewildered. But the truth is that the schoolma'am herself is the victim. The real villains are the quacks who now run the American school system . . . and they ruin her as a teacher. Every year she is beset by a series of new arcana and forced to struggle with them on penalty of losing her job. . . . As a result teaching becomes a madness and the children learn next to nothing.

Mencken was just one of the 20th century's trenchant opponents of public education. His friend and fellow "Tory anarchist," Albert Jay Nock, was skeptical about the possibility of universal education, especially in a state-run system. In his *Memoirs of a Superfluous Man*, Nock said the purpose of compulsory state education was to teach "the extreme of a hidebound nationalism and of a superstitious servile reverence for a sancrosanct State." It was also "a leveling agency, prescribing uniform modes of thought, belief, conduct, social deportment, diet, recreation, hygiene; an . . . inquisitorial body for the enforcement of these prescriptions, for nosing out heresies and irregularities and suppressing them."

Another critic was Isabel Paterson, a journalist and publicist of the Old Right. Her 1943 book, *The God of the Machine,* contained a chapter titled "Our Japanized Educational System,"[8] by which she meant that "progressive" education resembled Japan's system in which children are trained to submerge themselves in the group:

So in every way the natural outlet of energy in human beings, which in childhood is properly directed toward the development of intelligence and character, is choked down and subverted: the purpose of study is not to learn things which are true in themselves nor to develop independence through such knowledge, but to please and conform to arbitrary authority.

Noting that the schools are controlled by political power, she added:

There can be no greater stretch of arbitrary power than is required to seize children from their parents, teach them whatever the authorities decree they shall be taught, and expropriate from the parents the funds to pay for the procedure. If this principle really is not understood, let any parent holding a positive religious faith consider how it would seem to him if his children were taken by force and taught an opposite creed.

Paterson mocked the idea of "free education" as the "most absolute contradiction of facts by terminology of which the language is capable. Everything about such schools is compulsory, not free." She used the famous Scopes evolution trial of 1925 to illustrate how misunderstood that fact is. The state of Tennessee passed a law forbidding the teaching of Darwin's theory in the public schools. A teacher was prosecuted for violating the law. Many people ridiculed the Tennessee authorities—but for the wrong reasons.

Of course the law was absolutely improper; but it was attacked on the ground that the Darwinian theory of evolution is true, and that the Tennesseeans were uninformed yokels. But what if Darwinian evolution had been generally taught in the public schools of Tennessee, and a parent had tried to withhold his school taxes and refused to send his children to school *because he did not want them taught that theory*; how many of the ardent champions of Mr. Scopes would have defended such a parent? It is safe to say, not one. All they wanted was that the state should prescribe that their own particular scientific doctrine be taught, rather than an unorthodox creed. They were not the least concerned with freedom of thought, speech, or person. . . . In short, they did not question the political control of education; they only wanted to use it themselves. [Emphasis in original.]

Paterson understood that when the state controls education, it must control educational materials, such as textbooks. Thus, the variation that one would expect among private schools will not be found in a state monopoly system. Moreover, the inevitable and necessary selectivity will serve the sponsor of the educational system—the state. As she put it:

> Every politically controlled educational system will inculcate the doctrine of state supremacy sooner or later. . . . Once that doctrine has been accepted, it becomes an almost superhuman task to break the stranglehold of political power over the life of the citizen. It has had his body, property, and mind in its clutches from infancy. An octopus would sooner release its prey. A tax-supported, compulsory educational system is the complete model of the totalitarian state.

Paterson ended her chapter with a sharp question to the public school teacher who objects to the privatization of education: "Do you think nobody would willingly entrust his children to you or pay you for teaching them? Why do you have to extort your fees and collect your pupils by compulsion?"

Frank Chodorov, a great radical individualist, turned his attention to education in much of his writing. Like Paterson, he was concerned with the stultifying uniformity of state education and the indoctrination that must follow. "Can the tax-paid teacher," he asked in 1948, "even hint at the immorality of taxation? Can he void the glorification of political scoundrels in the school books? And now that we have gone in for state capitalism in a big way, how can he question the correctness of TVA [Tennessee Valley Authority], public housing or the monopoly of the mails?"[9] And like Paterson he debunked the idea that government schools are "free":

> In the full sense of the word, a free school is one that has no truck with the state, via its taxing powers. . . . What is known as "free education" is the least free of all, for it is a state-owned institution; it is socialized education—just like socialized medicine or the socialized post office—and cannot possibly be separated from political control. As for being "free" in the sense of being without cost, that is one of those imposter terms we like to use to hide ugly facts from ourselves; our public education is fully paid for, with all its deficiencies and inadequacies. And it

is paid for mainly by the poor, not the rich, because the poor in the aggregate constitute the largest segment of society and therefore pay the most in taxes.

Finally, he rejected the idea that public schools foster a free society. "This plausibility has obscured the fact that the public school is a political institution, and as such can be used for ends quite the opposite of freedom. For example, Hitler, Mussolini, and Stalin did not abolish the public school, but, rather, favored it as a necessary integral of their regimes. . . ."

Paterson and Chodorov have had widespread influence. The writings of each had a hand in stimulating creation of the modern libertarian, or radical individualist, movement that got under way after World War II. Two men who played key, early, and long-lasting roles in that movement, Leonard Read, founder of the Foundation for Economic Education, and F. A. Harper, founder of the Institute for Humane Studies, had a keen interest in education and were passionate opponents of the union of school and state.[10] Other opponents of state education and advocates of individual liberty who have been inspirations to libertarians in the postwar era are the late novelist-philosopher Ayn Rand, economist and historian Murray N. Rothbard, and philosopher John Hospers.[11]

There have been several important social critics who have concentrated their focus on education, among them Ivan Illich, author of the provocative *Deschooling Society,* and Paul Goodman, who wrote of *Compulsory Mis-education.* In his book, Illich writes, "The claim that a liberal society can be founded on the modern school is paradoxical. The safeguards of individual freedom are all canceled in the dealings of a teacher with his pupil." Education historians Joel Spring and E. G. West have done much to document the unattractive history of public schooling. In several books, Richard Mitchell, "the Underground Grammarian," has destroyed the mystique of the venerated schools of education, which provide the teachers for the public schools. No critic has gotten to the root of the poisonous tree of public education as John Holt has. Holt was a teacher in the finest private schools; he grew dissatisfied with what school per se required of him and his students. At first, he became a school reformer, hoping that if teachers understood children better, they would become better teachers. But eventually, he came to see school itself as the problem, and until his death in 1985, he promoted what he called "unschooling." For Holt, the problem with the public schools began with its compulsion. He wondered how children can explore the world when they are under state order to be in school. He saw compulsory attendance laws as a violation of individual freedom. In a letter written some years ago chiding the American Civil Liberties Union for not challenging those laws, Holt wrote that compulsory attendance seriously infringed on the civil liberties of children and parents. He noted that the ACLU would not tolerate laws that told adults that "on one hundred eighty days of the year, for six or more hours a day, you had to be at a particular place, and there do whatever people told you to do." And he rejected the argument that children may be treated that way because public policy aims at keeping them from ignorance. "But even if it were true that children were learning important things in schools and that they could not learn them anywhere else, neither of which I admit, I would still remind the ACLU that since in other more difficult cases, i.e., the Nazi rally in Skokie, Ill., it does not allow the needs of public policy to become an excuse for violating the basic liberties of its citizens, it ought not to in this case."[12]

Holt equally objected to other things the public schools did: keeping permanent records; keeping them secret from children and parents; opening the records to employers and the government; compulsory psychological testing; labeling children with such dubious terms as "hyperactive" and "learning disabled"; drugging children; assaulting children (euphemistically: corporal punishment), and more.

Holt had much to say about the nature of learning (see Chapter 5), but for him, freedom was fundamental to good education and good teaching. As he wrote:

> Only when all parents, not just rich ones, have a truly free choice in education, when they can take their children out of a school they don't like, and have a choice of many others to send them to, or the possibility of starting their own, or of educating their children outside of school altogether—only then will we teachers begin to stop being what most of us still are and if we are honest know we are, which is jailers and baby-sitters, cops without uniforms, and begin to be professionals, freely exercising an important valued, and honored skill and art.[13]

Holt is not the only teacher whose experience forced the conclusion that the public schools were incurably bad. That also describes John Taylor Gatto. He won national attention with the speeches he gave on being named New York City Teacher of the Year in 1990 and New York State Teacher of the Year in 1991.[14]

Before the New York State Senate, Gatto said:

We need to rethink the fundamental premises of schooling and decide *what* it is we want children to learn and *why*. For 140 years this nation has tried to impose objectives downward from a lofty command center made up of "experts," a central elite of social engineers. It hasn't worked. It won't work. And it is a gross betrayal of the democratic promise that once made this nation a noble experiment. The Russian attempt to create Plato's republic in Eastern Europe has exploded before our eyes; our own attempt to impose the same sort of central orthodoxy using the schools as an instrument is also coming apart at the seams, albeit more slowly and painfully. It doesn't work because its fundamental premises are mechanical, anti-human, and hostile to family life. Lives can be controlled by machine education but they will always fight back with weapons of social pathology: drugs, violence, self-destruction, indifference, and the symptoms I see in the children I teach.

In another speech, Gatto pointed out:

It is a great triumph of compulsory government monopoly mass-schooling that among even the best of my fellow teachers, and among even the best of my students' parents, only a small number can imagine a different way to do things. . . . Only a few lifetimes ago things were very different in the United States. . . . The promise of democracy was beginning to be realized. We turned our backs on this promise by bringing to life the ancient pharaonic dream of Egypt: compulsory subordination for all.

He also noted that it was inevitable that a large compulsory institution would devour our children, taking more and more of their time and leaving less and less for themselves. "School," he said, "takes our children away from any possibility of an active role in community life—in fact it destroys communities by relegating the training of children to the hands of certified experts—and by doing so it ensures our children cannot grow up fully human." He added that the discussion about national standards overlooks the obvious: "Schools teach exactly what they are intended to teach and they do it well: how to be a good Egyptian and remain in your place in the pyramid." No wonder, he said, that children turn to idleness, drugs, violence, suicide, and so on. "All the pathologies we've considered come about in large measure because the lessons of school prevent children from keeping important appointments with themselves and their families to learn lessons in self-motivation, perseverance, self-reliance, courage, dignity, and love."

The public school critics we've discussed had one thing in common: a belief that the future of our children depends on the separation of state and school. In the next chapter, we will speculate on what education might look like when that separation is accomplished.

Notes

[1] See George H. Smith, "Nineteenth-Century Opponents of State Education: Prophets of Modern Revisionism," in Robert R. Everhart, ed., *The Public School Monopoly: A Critical Analysis of Education and the State of American Society* (San Francisco: Pacific Research Institute, 1982).

[2] Wilhelm von Humboldt, *The Limits of State Action*, ed. J. W. Burrow (1792; Indianapolis, Ind.: Liberty Press, 1993). Quotations are from this book. Ironically, Humboldt in 1809 became Prussia's director for the Section for Public Worship and Education, in which capacity he oversaw the construction of the country's authoritarian public school system, which became a model for the American system (see Chapter 3). The historian Ralph Raico explains Humboldt's turnabout as a "patriotic" reaction to Prussia's ignominious defeat by Napoleon's army. See Ralph Raico, "Wilhelm von Humboldt," *New Individualist Review*, April 1961, pp. 18–22.

[3] Herbert Spencer, *Social Statics* (1850; New York: Robert Schalkenbach Foundation, 1970). This edition contains the important chapter "The Right to Ignore the State," which Spencer unfortunately removed from later editions. All quotations are from this edition.

[4] The essay appears in Auberon Herbert, *The Right and Wrong of Compulsion by the State and Other Essays*, ed. Eric Mack (Indianapolis: Liberty Classics, 1978).

[5] The economist Israel M. Kirzner makes a similar point about entrepreneurship in "The Perils of Regulation," in *Discovery and the Capitalist Process* (Chicago: University of Chicago Press, 1985).

[6] The Voluntaryist quotations that follow are from Smith's essay cited above.

[7] Unless otherwise noted, the Mencken quotations are found in Mayo DuBasky, ed., *The Gist of Mencken: Quotations from America's Critic* (Metuchen, N.J.: Scarecrow Press, 1990).

[8] Republished in 1993 by Transaction Publishers.

[9] Frank Chodorov, "Why Free Schools Are Not Free" and "Private Schools: The Solution to America's Educational Problem," in *Fugitive Essays: Selected Writings of Frank Chodorov*, ed. Charles H. Hamilton (Indianapolis: Liberty Press, 1980). All Chodorov quotations are from that volume.

[10] The Foundation for Economic Education is publisher of *The Freeman*, which has published many articles on free-market educa-

tion over the years. Some of the best of those articles have been compiled in *Public Education and Indoctrination* (Irvington-on-Hudson, N.Y.: Foundation for Economic Education, 1993).

[11] See Ayn Rand, *Capitalism: The Unknown Ideal* (New York: New American Library, 1967), pp. 89–92; Murray N. Rothbard, *For A New Liberty: The Libertarian Manifesto* (New York: Collier Books, 1978), pp. 119–141, and works cited in Chapters 2 and 3; and John Hospers, *Libertarianism: A Philosophy for Tomorrow* (Santa Barbara, Calif., Reason Press, 1971), pp. 374–85.

[12] John Holt, *Teach Your Own* (New York: Delacorte Press, 1981), pp. 19-20.

[13] John Holt, *What Do I Do Monday?* (New York: Dutton, 1970), p. 265.

[14] The speeches are reprinted in John Taylor Gatto, *Dumbing Us Down: The Hidden Curriculum of Compulsory Schooling* (Philadelphia: New Society Publishers, 1992). Gatto has left teaching since winning the awards.

5

Without Public Schools

People who live in Freedom will think with Freedom; but when the Mind is enslaved by fear, and the Body by chains, Inquiry and Study will be at an End.
—John Trenchard and Thomas Gordon
Cato's Letters[1]

The future of education, and of America as a free society, depends on the liberation of the American family from the grip of the public school. That may seem a needlessly drastic remedy. It is not. The schools are boring our kids to death—when they are not otherwise humiliating them, drugging them, or subjecting them to violence. They are teaching them that learning is to be equated with tedium, senseless tasks, arbitrary directives, a mindless competition for favor, and the stifling of curiosity. The public school system is an authoritarian, procrustean bureaucracy to which every child is expected to adjust himself. Ignoring the uniqueness of each individual, it expects all children of a given age to learn the same things at the same time in the same way. If a child does not meet expectations, the system assumes there is something wrong with *him,* not the school. Naturally, most students, if not humiliated and terrified, are bored. Patrick Welsh, a high school teacher in Alexandria, Virginia, one of the richest cities in the nation, writes that boredom is dominant at school. As Welsh put it:

> Instead of quality teaching, schools are obsessed with time and regimentation. Such a concern would be justifiable if it produced results, but what it produces is a feeling among students that if they show up and shut up, everything will be fine. . . .

81

Almost every student I talked to complained about the deadly repetition of course material over the years, especially history and some government courses.

Welsh quotes one student as saying, "The game is memorize this, spit it back and don't give me any grief." Another said, "It's hard to stay interested when you get the impression that administrators and teachers just want you to be there and keep on moving—that they don't care if you are interested as long as you aren't causing them any trouble." Bear in mind that these students are not from an inner-city school but attend one of the best high schools in suburbia. Welsh goes on to write, "A former teacher told me, only half joking, that most little boys in her elementary school were 'either labeled gifted and talented, or on Ritalin [the drug given to more and more kids who are diagnosed as having Attention Deficit Syndrome].'"[2]

That is what the public schools have brought us. It is time for that to end. Not another generation of children should be imprisoned in this misconceived system of so-called education.

The reformers

What can be done? There is a growth industry in educational reform, but despite the good intentions, most of the proposals miss the point. Take the charter school movement, for example. The charter school is a public school that is governed at the school level, free, theoretically, from the school bureaucracy. The hot word is "autonomy." But obviously, an autonomous public school is a contradiction in terms; there can be no such thing. Actually, it is more than a contradiction in terms; it is an oxymoron, the juxtaposition of two conflicting ideas for rhetorical effect. The effect sought here is the lulling of the public into thinking something is being done about the gross problems of the schools. No school can be autonomous as long as it is financed by taxation, filled by students compelled to be there, and subject to union, civil rights, and other regulations imposed by the state and federal governments. No school can be autonomous if it can't go out of business. And no one is proposing *that* for the public schools. But please note that the charter-school movement is a blunt admission that bureaucracy in education has failed.

Another reform idea that is getting lots of attention is "contracting out." In Baltimore, the city has hired Education Alternatives, Inc., to run several schools. The superintendent of the District of Columbia is interested in doing the same thing, but opposition from the school board and teachers' union has forced him to postpone the plan. Interest in such an idea is certainly a good sign. It is tantamount to the superintendent's saying, "I give up. We do not know how to run schools. So let's get a private company in here." But the solution is weak. The public school system would remain intact. Instead of directly employing managers for the schools, the school board would contract with managers. The board would still set educational objectives and other policies; the private firm would have jurisdiction only over means, not ends. Agreements with the teachers' union and other regulations would have to be honored by the contractor. Under some arrangements, the firm would collect a flat fee and wouldn't profit from cost savings. Thus, it would have no incentive to look for such savings. Since the board could choose not to renew the contract, the management firm would be subject to something resembling market forces. But we should not mistake "contracting out" for real market reform of the schools.

The other major reform proposal is the voucher plan. In broadest conception, it would take some of the money a school district now spends per pupil and give it to his parents in the form of a voucher. They could exchange the voucher for education at any public, private, or religious school. Parents and children need freedom of choice, but there are reasons to doubt that vouchers will achieve it. It is likely that before schools could accept vouchers, they would be required to meet a raft of standards that before long would make the private schools virtually indistinguishable from the public schools. There is already a precedent for that. Hillsdale College turns down all government aid and for that reason assumed that it was not obligated to abide by the federal government's myriad regulations. Not so, said the federal government. Since Hillsdale had students paying tuition with federal loans, it was indeed accepting federal money and thus had to follow the rules. The U.S. Supreme Court affirmed the government's position. Hillsdale's way out was to find private loans for such students so government money would not be needed. The analogy with vouchers is obvious. Schools will be able to remain free from government edict only by eschewing vouchers. But that will severely limit their clientele. The temptation will be to swallow the rules and take the vouchers. And there goes the private-school alternative.

Authors of voucher initiatives have tried to address that threat by including language to prohibit new regulations of private schools. California's unsuccessful 1993 initiative attempted to do that, although it would have permitted the state board of education to "require . . . each scholarship-redeeming school to choose and administer tests reflecting national standards for the purpose of measuring individual improvement." Even an airtight prohibition would present a problem. It would most likely harm an initiative's prospects for passage because, as the opposition would inevitably point out, the voucher plan would appear to authorize appropriation of "public" money to institutions not accountable to "public authorities." For taxpaying parents who would be controlling their own money, of course, that would not be true. But most voters will not see it that way. The opposition will persuade them that vouchers would obligate the government to support anyone who declares himself the administrator of a school. The upshot is that to the extent the voucher initiative insulates private schools from government regulation, it will suffer at the polls.

Besides, the voucher idea does not challenge what is fundamentally wrong with government involvement in education. People would still look to government for the financing of education. People who don't pay taxes, or who pay less than the value of the voucher, would still get a full voucher, expanding the current education entitlement to the private schools. Some voucher advocates go as far as to say that the plan will improve the public schools. Even if it could improve the schools, so what? Public education is objectionable in principle and necessarily inferior to a free-education market. If we could get better churches through subsidies, would that be reason to repeal the First Amendment? But vouchers won't improve the public schools. The theory is that parents will flock to private schools, pressuring the public schools to change or close. The problem is that public schools are not set up like private schools and do not act like them. Their response to competition will not be the same as that of a private school. Will public schools be allowed to "go out of business"? Not likely. Their administrators will rally the teachers' unions and other public employees to save them because "they can't be allowed to fail." And since the premises of state education will not have been challenged, the special interests will probably succeed. As Richard Mitchell has written:

> When we say, as we seem to more and more these days, that education in America is "failing," it is because we don't understand the institution. It is, in fact, succeeding enormously. It grows daily, hourly, in power and wealth, and that precisely *because* of our accusations of failure. The more we complain against it, the more it can lay claim to *our* power and wealth, in the name of curing those ills of which we complain.[3]

That said, well-meaning advocates of voucher, or school-choice, plans deserve credit for their concern about the thoroughly rotten deal that inner-city kids are getting in the public schools. The education establishment is strangling those children, and its knee-jerk opposition to any proposal that attempts to address that tragedy speaks volumes.

Beyond reform

Some voucher advocates concede the danger to the private schools, but wonder what else can be done to open alternatives to public schooling. We have to understand that nothing less than a frontal assault on the current system, a philosophical challenge to the premises of state education, will work. We can begin by revising our very conception of the purpose of education. Contrary to the educators, elected officials, and bureaucrats, our children are not a resource that the schools are mandated to develop for the good of the nation. In the words of Justice McReynolds in the landmark *Pierce v. Society of Sisters* (1925), "The child is not the mere creature of the state." He belongs to himself. We must reject the "compelling state interest" in our children asserted by government whenever parents refuse to toe the line. Education should not aim at making America "competitive" or at maintaining America's "global leadership." Parents and children should determine the nature and purpose of education. Learning to satisfy someone else is never as effective as learning to satisfy yourself.

Of course, part of any child's education should relate to the need to earn a living in the world's competitive marketplace. But that consideration is far different from treating education as a component of a grand strategy to enhance national competitiveness. Such a strategy turns America's children into cogs in the great national economic machine. That is a Prussian idea that should have never been imported to our shores in the 19th century. It is time to cast out that demon.[4]

Along with that, we will need a clarion call for the removal of all political barriers to self-education. The 19th-century individualist and abolitionist Gerrit Smith put it well when he said, "It is justice and not charity which the people need at the hands of government. Let government restore to them their land, and what other rights they have been robbed of, and they will then be able to pay for themselves—to pay their schoolmasters, as well as their parsons."

Today that sounds like a radical idea. Let people keep their own money, eliminate the bureaucratic barriers to spontaneous family and community activity—and people will see to their own education. If that sounds romantic and unrealistic, it only illustrates how far we have been taken in by the religion of state, which teaches that we, the benighted people, could not get along in even the simplest matters without our wise and benevolent governors. People taught their own children to read, write, and reckon for centuries without the help of government. But today we can't imagine how it could be done. And we call ourselves a free and independent people.

A free market in education

It is clear what needs to be done. For a start, all school taxes should be abolished. Multipurpose taxes—property, sales, and income taxes—should be reduced at least by the amount that currently goes to education. If other taxes cannot be done away with right away, they should be slashed drastically and soon. The personal income tax should be the first slated for repeal.[5] Most people could afford a good education for their children if government at all levels were not taking about 40 percent of their income.

The compulsory attendance laws in each state must also be abolished. Those laws violate the rights of families. They are also impractical. Keeping kids in school who don't want to be there hurts them as well as those who *do* want to be there. As the late John Holt and others have noted, forced attendance fundamentally transforms schools into jails. Students know they are there because they must be there. That has subtle, corrosive effects on students, teachers, and administrators. It is bad enough that many teachers convey to students the attitude that they are incapable of learning without help; the problem is compounded many times by the message of compulsory attendance laws: you may not leave. That, as Holt phrased it, puts the schools into the "jail business." One should not expect anyone to be both a good teacher and a good prison guard. Yet that is what is expected of teachers today, and the students know it.

Compulsory attendance laws were intended in part to keep children out of the workforce so that they would not compete with older workers. The state has no business telling people they cannot work simply because they are under 18 years old. That is a decision for kids and their parents.[6]

If the government requires children to attend school, it of course will assert the prerogative to define "school." That opens the door for government accreditation, academic standards, curriculum controls, standardized testing, and so on. If the compulsory attendance laws are repealed, the government would have no grounds to say what school is. That would open another door: to educational variety. One tragedy of government control of education is that we don't know what we've been missing. Many years ago, the self-styled experts designed "the one best system."[7] It was thought that there was no need for variety; anything else would be less than the best. The private schools for the most part were modeled on the public schools. Although the U.S. Supreme Court as far back as 1923 upheld the rights of parents to educate their children in alternative ways, government domination over education exercised a subtle control over private schools that kept them close copies of their public counterparts.[8] Moreover, since most people went through public schools or carbon-copy private schools, they came to believe that anything but the traditional method of education—teacher in front of age-graded class, grades, exams—was suspect. When it was time to educate their own children, they naturally sought schools like the ones they attended. Government schools thus stifled the market for education, not only by dominating it directly, but by smothering the demand for innovation.

With school taxes and compulsory attendance laws out of the way, education entrepreneurs would have free rein to offer alternatives. Anyone could open a school. There should be no regulations regarding curriculum or teacher qualifications, which are impediments to entrepreneurial discovery. The competitive market and the right of redress in cases of outright fraud would deter charlatans. Schools would be operated for profit. Schools would be nonprofit. Schools would be church-related. Schools would be secular. Schools would be independent. Schools would be part of chains. Schools would be set up by employers to make it attractive for their parents to take jobs. The public war over values would finally be over, because no one would be compelled to support beliefs he did not hold. Parents would be free to bring their children up in their own philosophy or religion—and choose their schools accordingly. At that point, the words of Supreme Court Justice Robert Jackson would be realized, "If there is any fixed star in our constitutional constellation, it is that no official, high or petty, can prescribe what shall be orthodox in politics, nationalism, religion, or other matters of opinion or force citizens to confess by word or act their faith therein."[9]

We can be certain that there would be the widest variety of schools. Obviously, we cannot know in detail what new ideas education entrepreneurs will come up with. That would require us to see into the future, and that is impossible. We live in an open-ended universe. We don't know all that we will know tomorrow. Knowledge and techniques are discovered on the spot, not in an ivory tower but in the bustle of the competitive marketplace. That would be true of educational techniques also. The economist Israel M. Kirzner teaches that where government regulation rules out profit opportunities, we should not expect entrepreneurial discovery.[10] But where there is freedom to garner profit, we can expect what Kirzner calls "utter surprise," the serendipity of discovering knowledge that no one anticipated. Bureaucrats are notoriously bad at entrepreneurship for a simple reason: they do not stand to capture entrepreneurial profit as a reward for discovery. That is why, regardless of what the test scores are at any given moment, a government educational system will always be inferior to a free-market educational system.

What has been lacking in the education field is the "utter surprise" of finding better ways of doing things. If education entrepreneurs did not have to worry about running afoul of government school officials, they would be liberated in their ability to innovate and find better methods of helping children learn. A distinction must be made between the entrepreneurial process and what may appear to be a similar process involving education bureaucrats. In recent decades, the school bureaucracy has passed through several fads, including the New Math, open classrooms, back to basics, and now, as part of the new national standards passed by Congress, a proposal that each student master one of the arts.[11] Such ersatz innovation has nothing in common with entrepreneurial innovation for a simple reason: unlike entrepreneurs, bureaucrats don't have customers— they have taxpayers and captive students. That makes a world of difference. The bureaucrats come to see themselves as social engineers and the students as their subjects. (The National Education Association once distributed a bumper sticker calling itself—shudder—the "United Mind Workers.") The bureaucrats will be tempted to test out the latest vogue theories that emanate from educational psychology, social psychology, and sociology, much as psychologists experiment with laboratory animals. Private-school entrepreneurs do not approach their customers in that manner. They face a harsh reality-check: consenting clients and the profit-and-loss statement. If parents don't like an innovation and the school persists, they can pull their children out and go elsewhere.

Invoking the profit-and-loss statement could cause some people to fear that free-market schools would cater to the lowest common denominator. David Guterson, in an otherwise excellent book, fears privatization of education because:

> such a system readily lends itself to profiteers eager to exploit families out of greed. A nation of private schools will rapidly devolve into a nation of chain educational franchises offering

McLearning in lieu of real learning, feathered out with slick advertisements and late-summer enrollment specials. Educational subsidiaries of major corporations will dictate not only what sort of schools we have but—even more disturbing—our very conception of the possibilities of education. We will lose, with time, our ability to discern the good.[12]

It is sad that a book dedicated to the good judgment of parents suddenly starts to patronize them like an elitist education bureaucrat. As David Boaz points out, when people express doubts about parents' ability to choose good schools, they are not thinking of white, middle-class suburbanites. They (though perhaps not Guterson) are thinking of blacks in the inner cities. In other words, there is at least an implicit racism lurking in their doubts. Boaz argues that there will be good, inexpensive schools even if only a few parents are able to identify a good school. Just as a small number of savvy grocery shoppers induce supermarkets to offer value to *all* shoppers, he writes, so "a small number of educated consumers will force all suppliers to compete for *their* business, thereby providing reasonable combinations of price and quality for all their customers."[13] Even if charlatans offer the kinds of "schools" Guterson anticipates, it is not at all clear that many parents would send their kids to them. Since there are few economies of scale in education and little capital is needed to set up and run a good school (see Marva Collins's success in Chicago[14]), bad schools would readily be confronted by competition.

As noted, we cannot predict in any detail what would arise in a free market in education. But we do know that over the past decade, computer and telecommunications technology has changed in a way highly relevant to education. Today people have on their desks—or in their briefcases—computing power that only a few years ago none but the largest companies could afford. The price continues to fall. The development of huge databases, modems, on-line services, interactive compact disks, and virtual reality is bringing a literal world of information into our homes. Homes and classrooms can now be linked, enabling students to "attend" the classes of their choice thousands of miles away. Right now, encyclopedias on compact disk display motion pictures of recent historical events. Soon the desktop computer will be able to display the books of the greatest libraries and high-resolution pictures from the world's greatest museums. The possibilities are endless. It's all the product of the free market, human intelligence, and sand (from which are made silicon chips and fiber-optic cables).[15]

Author Lewis J. Perelman provides a taste of what is coming:

> Eleven-year-old Jessie is sitting at a multimedia computer reading some text about the Civil War in an encyclopedia program. She comes to a mention of General Burnside. Curious to know who he was, she points at his name on the screen with a mouse and clicks. The "button" zips the screen instantly to another file—represented as a card in a stack of index cards, or as a page in a book—with biographical information about Burnside. Among other things, Jessie learns that "sideburns" were named after the way he wore his whiskers, and that he composed the bugle call, "Taps," and hears a recording of the tune. Or, clicking on a mention of the Battle of Fredericksburg, she might view a sequence from a movie about the battle. . . . In just a few years, our young friend Jessie won't be bound to a desktop to use powerful multimedia tools to nurture her curiosity about General Burnside and the Civil War. On vacation with her family in Fredericksburg, Virginia, she could carry a Discman-sized knowledge box that would answer her questions about "Taps" and the general's whiskers while she tours the battlefield. A decade or so into the future, she wouldn't have to tote a bulky box. Even more powerful knowledge technology will fit in a wristwatch or, better, a pair of smart eyeglasses that respond to voice requests, and that could project holographic images of maps or simulated troop movements over the vista of the real battleground before her.[16]

How could education ever be the same? Can we expect such innovation from the government? Of course not. Think of Federal Express. Think of the fax. Think of electronic mail. Now think of the U.S. Postal Service. You get the idea. We cannot have our children held back by post-office-style schools.

Is school per se the problem?

Given freedom, parents and children may well discover that what's wrong with government schools is not just that they are *government* schools but that they are government *schools*. They may figure out, to paraphrase Mark Twain, that school gets in the way of education. At least 300,000 children and their parents in the United States, and by some estimates up to a million and a half, have decided that is the case; they refuse to go to any school at all. Homeschooling is gaining a prominence it hasn't had since the public schools were established a century and a half ago. Some homeschoolers, at least in the beginning, re-create the classroom at home, operating on a rigid schedule, using tests, and following the traditional age-grade system. But a growing number eschew the trappings of school. Strictly speaking, they are not homeschoolers. They are, to use John Holt's term, *un*schoolers.

Why do they reject school? Because they believe that school is inimical to real learning. By learning, they do not mean memorization of what someone else thinks is important until the exam is completed. They mean the authentic understanding that comes from an internal desire to know. The traditional classroom seems an odd place to learn. Patrick Welsh, the public school teacher quoted above, asks adults to take a fresh look at the classroom:

> Imagine an office where you sit at a desk and do the same work as 25 co-workers. No one is allowed to talk. At the end of 50 minutes, a bell rings, and whether you're finished or not, you must immediately move to another office, have a different boss and different colleagues—and start a job that had nothing to do with what you were just working on. Imagine doing that six or seven times a day. That is the essence of the environment that educators have designed for teenagers full of energy and raging hormones.[17]

Younger children face a similar environment. Bursting with curiosity about the world around them, including their fellow pupils, they are ordered to sit still, keep quiet, and don't touch. That is called "socialization." If they cannot follow orders, they may be diagnosed as having attention deficit disorder and drugged or may be declared "learning disabled," a label that will follow them throughout life. As Holt explained, schools implicitly (and sometimes explicitly) teach children that learning can take place only when they are shut away from the world with children their own age in a special place and are under the direction of a specially trained adult. The children are empty vessels into which the teacher pours knowledge. The implicit message is that what they have been doing for the first several years of their lives has not been learning, but something rather less important: playing. Of course, during that time they have done one of the toughest things they will ever do: they have learned their parents' language. They have also learned to stand, walk, run, observe countless customs, and in many cases read, write, count, and do arithmetic. They did it all, incidentally, without the help of a specially trained adult and with little or no formal instruction at all. Holt once said that if children were taught to speak the way schools teach reading, children would talk the way many of them read. (The NEA had another bumper sticker that showed its arrogance and propensity to propagandize: "If you can read this, thank a teacher." Many children teach themselves to read. The NEA doesn't say whom to blame if you can't read.) The schools teach children that the way they have been learning is illegitimate, that real learning must be tedious, unpleasant, and sometimes humiliating. Some lesson![18]

As Holt, a former teacher, wrote:

> The schools assume that children are not interested in learning and are not much good at it, that they will not learn unless made to, that they cannot learn unless shown how, and that the way to make them learn is to divide up the prescribed material into a sequence of tiny tasks to be mastered one at a time, each with its appropriate morsel and shock. And when this method doesn't work, the schools assume there is something wrong with the children—something they must diagnose and treat. All these assumptions are wrong.[19]

Home-schoolers (or *un*schoolers) have come to understand that children learn all the time and that the apparent separation of life's activities into learning and nonlearning is self-defeating. Children learn from everything they do. What's the point of making education compulsory when it is inevitable? (It would be like making observance of the law of gravity compulsory.) That does not mean that children require no guidance. But it says a lot about what the guidance should consist of and who is best at providing it.

In school, one teacher attempts to impose learning on 25 or more children whom he barely knows, using threats and rewards (grades) to get his way. The children, although of the same age, differ in knowledge and ability. Yet the teacher cannot tailor his methods to each child, whose requirements may differ vastly from the other children. He is on a rigid schedule and must cover a prescribed lesson plan within a prescribed time. The brightest and most advanced quickly become bored. The slowest become frustrated and frightened. Those in between become complacent. There's little chance for the digressions that children's curiosity demands. What the children soon learn is that success depends on giving the teacher what he wants. They learn all the devices for currying favor; they "game" the system. Those who rebel against that game become the troublemakers.

The system has the defining characteristic of a bureaucracy: the "main concern is to comply with the rules and regulations, no matter whether they are reasonable or contrary to what was intended."[20] And there are so many rules. You cannot talk without permission. You cannot get up, or get a drink of water, or go to the bathroom without permission. If you miss a class or a day, you must have a "good" excuse. It sounds like preparation for citizenship in a totalitarian state. As Richard Mitchell puts it, "The explicit principle of American schooling for the last sixty years or so [is] the belief that the purpose of education is to bring about a certain kind of society, and that the individual benefits from education to the degree in which he is adjusted to that society."[21]

But, some will say, you can't have a school without those rules. Grades are necessary to get the students to do the work and for tracking. And if the kids could come and go as they please, they'd never be in class. What does that tell us? It is certainly true that a traditional classroom requires rules. It is the convenience of the school, not learning, that requires them. The rules do not conduce learning; they get in the way. What makes the rules necessary is the fact that two dozen or more children are packed together with one teacher. As Ron Harrington, a teacher, says, the reason schools don't work is that they are filled with children—curious, energetic kids. Put 20 of them together and a lot will happen: but little of it is what most people would call real academic learning.

Moreover, what is taught is detached from the children's lives. It has to be that way because school is detached from real life. It has an inherent artificiality to it. As Holt wrote:

> We can best help children, not by deciding what we think they should learn and thinking of ingenious ways to teach them, but by making the world, as far as we can, accessible to them, paying serious attention to what they do, answering their questions— if they have any—and helping them explore the things they are most interested in.[22]

Those who might associate Holt's philosophy with the romanticism and primitivism of Jean-Jacques Rousseau should consult the work of Herbert Spencer. As we saw in Chapter 4, Spencer, who was committed to reason as well as individualism, strongly opposed government control of education. He also had many positive things to say about how learning should occur. In one of his essays on education, he wrote:

> [A principle] which cannot be too strenuously insisted upon, is, that in education the process of self-development should be

encouraged to the fullest extent. Children should be led to make their own investigations, and to draw their own inferences. They should be *told* as little as possible, and induced to *discover* as much as possible. Humanity has progressed solely by self-instruction. . . . Those who have been brought up under the ordinary school-drill, and have carried away with them the idea that education is practicable only in that style, will think it hopeless to make children their own teachers. If, however, they will call to mind that the all-important knowledge of surrounding objects which a child gets in its early years is got without help—if they will remember that the child is self-taught in the use of its mother tongue—if they will estimate the amount of that experience of life, that out-of-school wisdom, which every boy gathers for himself. . . they will find it a not unreasonable conclusion, that if the subjects be put before him in right order and right form, any pupil of ordinary capacity will surmount his successive difficulties with but little assistance. . . . This need for perpetual telling is the result of our stupidity, not of the child's.[23]

Spencer, sounding much like Holt, warned against using threats and punishment to force a child to learn what he doesn't wish to learn, for that will "produce . . . a disgust for knowledge in general" and turn him into "a mere passive recipient of our instruction." Further, Spencer proposed as a test of any educational method the following: "Does it create a pleasurable excitement in the pupils?" He recommended scrapping an apparently sound method if it bores a child because his "intellectual instincts are more trustworthy than our reasonings." As he put it, "In respect to the knowing faculties, we may confidently trust in the general law, that under normal conditions, healthful action is pleasurable, while action which gives pain is not healthful."

Anyone who doubts Holt's and Spencer's approach to learning should examine their own lives: of the important things one understands about the world, what proportion was learned in school? What proportion was self-taught?

Family-based learning—homeschooling is a misnomer because it wrongly suggests isolation—provides the best environment for self-teaching. No one knows a child better or cares more about him than his parents. No one is in a better position to accommodate a child's unique needs and abilities. The one-to-one "student-teacher ratio" permits instant feedback and immediate adjustment. In other words, the efficiency, as well as the efficacy, of such learning is nonpareil. That explains why family-based learners outperform schooled children in every study.[24] Moreover, family-based learning is the best—probably the only—way to fully respect how learning is embedded in everyday living. This is not to deny the value of formal instruction. Homeschoolers routinely patronize piano teachers, French instructors, dance studios, and Tae Kwon Do *dojangs*. That does not violate the principles we are discussing. They do so by choice and with the understanding that learning some things requires the help of people with specialized knowledge or skills. The so-called basics, however, are not among those things.

Family-based learning provides the opportunity for parents and children to declare their independence from the state's educational system. They need not wait for any reforms. They can do it at once. Of course, the abolition of school taxes and a major reduction in the general burden of government would make it easier for families to turn to that form of education. The government's monetary inflation of the 1970s forced many unwilling mothers to leave home in search of a paycheck. They and their children have suffered for it. That's another government policy to thank for the decline of the family. In an economy unburdened by government, rising productivity would enable one earner to support a family. If needed, supplemental income could be produced from within the home; such opportunities have been greatly expanded by new technologies, such as home computers and desktop publishing, which in turn have made "telecommuting"—working at home—possible. In other words, family-based learning is not as difficult or as financially costly as people might think. As its practitioners can attest, the rewards are immense. It's a matter of priorities.[25]

The key political issue, however, is not schooling or unschooling, but educational freedom. Regardless of motives, the people who foisted state education on us have committed a grave offense. But bygones are bygones. Our concern must be with the future, with our children. Using a variety of strategies, we must reclaim the right to raise our children and to help them educate themselves. In a fundamental sense, that is the American way. That freedom and responsibility has been usurped long enough. It is time for us to change things. It is time that a wall of separation be erected between school and state.

Notes

[1] *Cato's Letters* were a series of popular revolutionary libertarian essays circulated in England in the 1720s and later in the American colonies. They are credited with seeding the American intellectual soil with radical Lockean political philosophy and making the Revolution possible. See Bernard Bailyn, *The Ideological Origins of the American Revolution* (Cambridge, Mass.: Harvard University Press, 1967).

[2] Patrick Welsh, "The Bored of Education: An Apology from a Teacher, *The Washington Post*, "Outlook" section, June 21, 1992.

[3] Richard Mitchell, *The Graves of Academe* (New York: Fireside/ Simon & Schuster, 1981), p. 4.

[4] Regarding training for global competition: with the technological world changing as fast as it now does, a good education does not consist in learning a particular body of knowledge; the rate of obsolescence is too great. Rather, what counts is, in Holt's words, "resourcefulness, flexibility, curiosity, skill in learning, readiness to unlearn." Schools are notoriously bad at imparting those virtues. That point is also made by Elizabeth Hoffman in "How Can Displaced Workers Find Better Jobs?" in Donald N. McCloskey, ed., *Second Thoughts: Myths and Morals of U.S. Economic History* (New York: Oxford University Press, 1993), p. 62.

[5] Although income tax rates were lowered in the 1980s, over the years, the federal government has taken advantage of inflation, which constituted a tax increase through "bracket creep" and erosion of the personal exemption. If the personal exemption that taxpayers may claim for themselves and their children had kept pace with inflation, today it would be worth over $8,000. Until the tax is repealed, taxpayers should at least be able to exclude education expenses from their taxable income. See Roy E. Cordato and Sheldon Richman, "A Tax Deduction for Education," *The Freeman*, June 1994, pp. 303–305.

[6] Child labor has been subject to many myths. See Clark Nardinelli, *Child Labor and the Industrial Revolution* (Bloomington, Ind.: Indiana University Press, 1990).

[7] See David Tyack, *The One Best System* (Cambridge, Mass.: Harvard University Press, 1974).

[8] On the Court's recognition of parental rights over their children's education, see John W. Whitehead and Wendell R. Bird, *Home Education and Constitutional Liberties*, 2nd edition revised, (Westchester, Ill.: Crossway Books, 1984). See also the excellent book by Stephen

Arons, *Compelling Belief: The Culture of American Schooling* (New York: New Press/McGraw Hill, 1983).

[9] *West Virginia v. Barnette*, 1943; quoted in Arons, p. 209.

[10] See Israel M. Kirzner, "The Perils of Regulation," in his *Discovery and the Capitalist Process* (Chicago: University of Chicago Press, 1985).

[11] The national standards, known as "Goals 2000," are "voluntary." That is, states and local school districts must adopt them only if they want federal money.

[12] David Guterson, *Family Matters: Why Homeschooling Makes Sense* (New York: Harcourt Brace, 1992), p. 197.

[13] David Boaz, ed., *Liberating Schools: Education in the Inner City* (Washington, D.C.: Cato Institute, 1991), p. 34.

[14] See among others, Rita Kramer, "Marva Collins and American Public Education, *The American Spectator*, April 1993, pp. 8–13.

[15] So much for the idea that resources are "natural" and capable of being depleted. Nature provides only stuff; human ingenuity transforms stuff into a resource, just as it turned sand into an information revolution that rivals the industrial revolution. See Julian Simon, *The Ultimate Resource* (Princeton, N.J.: Princeton University Press, 1981), and many works by Peter Bauer for details.

[16] Lewis J. Perelman, *School's Out: Hyperlearning, The New Technology, and the End of Education* (New York: Morrow, 1992), pp. 43–44.

[17] Welsh.

[18] Holt makes another interesting point: strictly speaking, children don't *learn* to walk and talk in the sense of explicitly acquiring skills and practicing. They simply walk and talk in pursuit of their objectives. They may not do it well at first. But as far as they are concerned, they do not begin in a learning stage and move to a doing stage. See Holt, *Instead of Education* (Boston: Pinchpenny Press/Holt Associates, 1976), p. 14.

[19] John Holt, *Learning All the Time: How Small Children Begin to Read, Write, Count, and Investigate the World Without Being Taught* (Reading, Mass.: Addison-Wesley, 1989), pp. 151–52.

[20] Ludwig von Mises, *Bureaucracy* (1944; New Rochelle, N.Y.: Arlington House, 1969), p. 41.

[21] Richard Mitchell, *The Leaning Tower of Babel* (New York: Fireside/Simon & Schuster, 1984), p. 136.

[22] *Learning All the Time*, p. 162.

[23] Spencer wrote four essays on education between 1854 and 1859. They have been compiled as *Education, Intellectual, Moral and Physical* (Paterson, N.J.: Littlefield Adams, 1963). See pp. 124–28.

[24] See Guterson; see also John W. Whitehead and Alexis Irene Crow, *Home Education: Rights and Reasons* (Wheaton, Ill.: Crossway Books, 1993), pp. 137ff.

[25] My own family discovered this when we became disenchanted with our eldest daughter's elementary school. All three children are now unschooled, while my wife, Kathleen, earns income at home through desktop publishing.

6

Conclusion

Education—compulsory schooling, compulsory learning—is a tyranny and a crime against the human mind and spirit. Let all those escape it who can, any way they can.

—John Holt

This book has argued the following:

1. Political and economic theory offers ample evidence that government-run schools must be inimical to the interests of people seeking real education. Since they are coercively financed and administered—and since their students are compelled to attend—government schools will necessarily be bureaucratic and procrustean: the "one best system." Since public schools interject government into sensitive areas, such as education in values, the system necessarily encroaches on the prerogatives of families and breaches the wall of separation between church and state.

2. The architects of public schooling in the United States believed that government had a "compelling interest" in molding children into Good Citizens according to a grand plan. Indeed, that idea has been intrinsic to public schooling since the time of Sparta. The founders of the modern American system of public education were moved by the vision of national education in authoritarian Prussia, whose system was explicitly designed to serve the military and civil-service interests of the bureaucratic state. They saw public schooling as a way of creating a national culture, eliminating poverty and crime, moderating religious and other differences, and keeping children out of the workforce. The key was compulsory attendance. Children, in short, existed for the benefit and future of the nation.

3. Radical individualists and libertarians have made principled criticisms of public schooling from the beginning. They opposed coercive financing through taxation and compulsory attendance. They pointed out that the administrators of government schools do not have the same interests as the parents and children who must use them. They argued that government schools would inevitably be propaganda mills designed to indoctrinate children in the religion of the state and turn them into loyal taxpayers and soldiers. In place of public schools, they proposed the absolute separation of school and state, freeing parents and children to look after education on their own.

4. A free market in education would feature wide variety, the details of which cannot be foreseen. The entrepreneurial discovery process would have full rein, and people would be free to start and patronize any kind of school. A free market would unleash on behalf of education the creativity that is evident in high technology and other areas of the marketplace. The clash over values that has been fought out in the public schools would end; parents and children would decide for themselves what kind of moral and intellectual education is appropriate.

As shown in the Appendix, there are many empirical indications that the public schools are in bad shape. Test scores, students unprepared for the world of work, crime, irrelevant subjects, and a general process of "dumbing down" have all combined to create the greatest disenchantment with American public schooling in 150 years. While the people are upset, the education bureaucrats and their boosters insist that the problems are not systemic and can be corrected—with more money from the taxpayers.

The libertarian alternative proposed here would return child-raising authority and education to parents. Unfortunately, that is what bothers many people about that alternative. The statist intellectual elite, statist-liberal and conservative, believe that most parents are incapable of raising their children. That is why they seek to extend public schooling as much as possible, through early day care, year-round school, long evenings of homework, and so on. The more the schools have the children, the less the parents have them—and the less they have themselves. This issue is fundamental: who will raise the children? The elite have not yet had the courage to extend their views logically. If most parents are not capable of overseeing the education of their children, maybe they are incompetent in other respects, as well. Should the state certify the competency of people before they may become parents? That idea is not far from what some already believe. No one in the United States has advocated such a monstrous state intervention. But one cannot help but feel that the reason lies not in principle but in public relations. (Maybe such a proposal will be offered in the name of stopping nonexistent "over-population.")

Some educators would prohibit homeschooling, if not altogether, at least in cases where the parents are not certified to teach. Since 1988 the National Education Association has annually passed a resolution against homeschooling, claiming that it cannot provide a "comprehensive education experience." The teachers union would require teacher certification of parents and state approval of home curricula. "Education isn't just cramming facts into kids, it's learning to work with others," says Gary Watts, director of the NEA's National Center for Innovation. "I think most homeschool advocates miss what school's all about."

The decline of the family is lamented by people of many political stripes—even the NEA. How curious, then, that most intellectuals, whether statist-liberal or conservative, still have not discovered the public school's role in subverting family. No one among them advocates removing the state entirely from education and turning the matter fully over to families. Statist-liberals seek a still more intrusive state role, but so do most conservative intellectuals, who push for national standards and a single curriculum. Both sides are so imbued with the religion of the state that they can find a solution to the education crisis only in government.

Thus, genuine advocates of liberty have an important role to play, for it is not being played by anyone else. Libertarians and radical individualists must explicitly apply to education the glorious principle of liberty: the liberty of individuals and their families to raise their children without interference by the state. That is the key to solving the crisis of education and the crisis of values that so bedevils the American people. The ceding of responsibility to government has brought us to our present condition. Only by taking back that responsibility can we have any hope for a happy and prosperous future. The issue is liberty, and libertarians must not shrink from pointing that out. It is time to end the dead hand of state education. It is time to separate school and state . . . and liberate America's families.

Appendix:
The State of Public Schools

The overwhelming evidence shows that American schools have never achieved more than they currently achieve.

—Gerald Bracey

Much ink has been dedicated to the question of whether the public schools have deteriorated from some earlier, superior condition. That, as will be shown, is not as simple an issue as it first appears. Some things are not easily measured. But that is not the most critical question to ask. What should concern the American people is not whether the schools are worse but whether they are good. This is elementary. Should it matter that they are not worse if they are also not good? If earlier generations unwittingly settled for too little in the matter of education, should that bind the current generation? While the tireless debate over the quality of the schools today versus the quality of those of thirty years ago can yield some useful material, it is no substitute for the task of asking: What is the point of education, and is it being fulfilled?

How are the public schools doing?

There is a hearty literature on just how well the schools are performing their job. It is a small matter to find vigorous advocates on either side of the question, and the debate is often acrimonious. In analyzing the debate, it is first necessary to decide which measuring rod or rods to use. Drop-out rate? SAT scores? Teacher-student ratios? Per-pupil spending? The argument over how to measure educational quality is as fiercely contentious as the argument over quality itself. There are less obvious indicators, as well. For example, what is learned from the fact that, according to studies done in the 1980s, public school teachers in some of the nation's major cities send their children to private schools in percentages ranging from 20 percent (Dallas-Ft. Worth) to 50 percent (Milwaukee)?[1] Later figures are not yet available. But who would bet money that the percentages are lower? Keith Geiger, president of the National Education Association, said that nationally 40 percent of urban public school teachers with school-age children send their children to private school.[2] Denis Philip Doyle, who has studied this matter, points out that in New Orleans's center city, 52 percent of teachers send their children to private schools. In Nashville, the proportion is 40 percent; in Albuquerque, 30; and in Charlotte, 25.[3] Of course, we should expect that more public-school teachers would choose private school for their children if they could afford it. It is a given that when parents become affluent enough, they move their children to private schools.

Another indicator that cannot be ignored is the perception of employers. Those are the people whose living depends on finding qualified employees for their companies. Their vantage point enables them to see the results of public schooling up close. What do they think? According to a 1991 Harris Education Research Center survey, just 33 percent could say that recent high school graduates have "the ability to read and understand written and verbal instructions"; 25 percent reported that graduates are "capable of doing arithmetic functions." The Harris survey commented that "this means that most employers have serious doubts about the functional capability of much of the labor pool from which they must find new employees."[4]

The survey also found that less than one-third of employers could agree that recent graduates could read well; 22 percent thought they had learned mathematics well; and only 12 percent thought they had learned how to write well.[5]

Every bit as significant is that no more than 30 percent give a positive rating to recent students "having the capacity to concentrate on the work done over an extended period of time," that only 25 percent say they are "motivated to give all they have to the job they are doing," that 20 percent feel they "have a real sense of dedication to work," that only 19 percent feel recent students "have real discipline in their work habits," and that 10 percent feel recent students have "learned to solve complex problems." All of these attributes, of course, are critical elements in achieving a high level of performance on the job.[6]

The authors of the survey commented that employers find that recent high school graduates are "by and large borderline in terms of functional literacy, their capacity to express themselves, and their basic functional skills. . . . In short, in the view of employers, recent graduates' education has at best prepared them marginally for work."[7]

To address these deficiencies, some companies are having to turn to remedial services in math, reading, and writing. The Harris survey found that 28 percent of employers have increased such services over the past five years. But only 18 percent say the remedial services work. "Thus," states the survey report, "46% of all employers say their rate of retention of new hires has been diminishing. Indeed, 69% say the number of high school graduates they have to screen before finding those 'who can meet our standards of employment' has risen. For every one acceptable applicant, they find they have to reject *five* others."[8]

Similar frustration with the quality of education was reported in a 1991 study by the National Association of Manufacturers. Forty percent of 360 small, medium, and large manufacturers said the poor quality of employees holds them back from upgrading technology; 37 percent have difficulty improving productivity; and 30 percent say they cannot give their employees more responsibility.[9]

While these and other studies yield consistent results, they have their critics. The critics say that employers have always disparaged the skills of employees and that such comments do not reflect on the quality of their education. Joseph Gibbons, who wrote the NAM study, points out that surveys may be biased by the fact that more applicants than in the past speak accented English and perhaps not much English at all. "I'm wondering if an awful lot of the smaller manufacturers are not asking for carbon copies of themselves when they were entering the workforce," said Gibbons.[10]

It is true that people have a tendency to think that the good old days were better than the present in most ways. That could shape the thinking of many employers about the current crop of young recruits. On the other hand, employers have a big incentive to be looking out for their businesses. Their complaints should not be discounted.

Their complaints sound rather similar to those voiced by college teachers. The Carnegie Foundation surveyed them in 1989 and found that 67 percent indicated "a widespread lowering of standards in American higher education. Seventy-five percent described their students as "seriously underprepared in basic skills."[11]

105

The test data

The subjective impressions of the qualifications of high school graduates are amply buttressed by data, namely test scores and other performance indicators. Economist William A. Niskanen, for example, points out that the percentage of teenagers completing high-school on time has been about the same for the last twenty years. Moreover, there has been a 3 to 4 percent increase in the number of high school graduates enrolled in college or completing one or two years of college. But Niskanen also points out that 25 percent of college freshman in 1984 were taking at least one remedial course, and enrollment in remedial classes increased by at least 10 percent a year from 1978 to 1984 in 63 percent of colleges. That record led Niskanen to conclude "that the high schools have maintained a roughly constant graduation rate only by tolerating an erosion in the quality of schooling in the basic subjects."[12]

This erosion is evident in the trend set by the scores of American high school students on the Scholastic Aptitude Test and the American College Test, which test problem-solving skills and substantive understanding, respectively. In his analysis, Niskanen points out that making sense of the score trends is not simple because of several factors. First, a larger percentage of high-school students take these tests now than in the past; thus, the composite scores could understate performance. But, Niskanen notes, more and more schools "teach to the tests," and many students prepare for the test through formal preparatory courses. So the test scores could overstate average performance.[13]

At any rate, composite scores on both tests dropped from 978 in 1963 to 890 in 1980. After a slight recovery, to 904, by the mid 1980s, the scores have held steady.[14] Moreover, over the last thirty years, the SAT grading system has become more lenient, according to social scientists Charles Murray and R. J. Herrnstein.[15] Yet in the seventies and eighties, writes Niskanen, the public schools increased spending per student a great deal. In other words, the recent increase in public-school spending, the average of which in constant dollars has gone from $2,035 per pupil in 1960 to $5,247 in 1990, has accomplished no more than a halt in the decline in test scores.[16]

Is the decline in scores explainable by the fact that more students are taking the exam than ever before? Is "democratization" the reason for the decline? Murray and Herrnstein do not think so. They write that the democratization explanation is misleading. They infer from the SAT data that, while the educational aptitude of American high schoolers overall has not worsened since the 1950s, "the SAT decline was real and large for the students who take the SAT, meaning that the decline was real for America's most capable young people." "The culprit is not the democratization of the SAT population but rather the 'mediocritization' of the college track in high school—our term for the downward trend of the educational skills of America's academically most promising youngsters toward those of the average student."[17]

They report that two studies that began in the 1950s fail to indicate that high school students on the whole perform more poorly in math and verbal tests than they did before the SAT-score decline. But the fall and stagnation in SAT scores do indeed indicate that the best students are worse off than they were before 1963. That deterioration, they write, cannot be attributed to increased participation by minority students (including Asian-Americans, who score better than whites on the math test) or poor, white students. In fact, looking just at the white population, the surge in participation in the SAT actually began in the 1950s and early 1960s, not in the late 1960s. "In other words, contrary to the democratization thesis, the first decade of the dramatically increased participation in the SAT saw *no* decline in scores. Then in the late 1960s, again contrary to conventional wisdom, the proportion of high school students taking the SAT began to shrink."[18]

Murray and Herrnstein note that their interpretation of the data is consistent with Daniel J. Singal's documentation of a 40 percent drop, between 1972 and 1983, in the proportion of students scoring over 600 in the SAT verbal exam (from 11.4 to 6.9 percent) and a decline in SAT scores for freshmen at many of the best colleges in the United States. A decline in the proportion scoring over 600 in math was reversed by the mid 1980s. The proportion of 700+ scores fell too from 1972 to 1981; but while the decline in the math test rebounded, the decline in the verbal test did not. Murray and Herrnstein add that the improvement occurs among whites and so cannot be explained by the presence of Asian-Americans.[19] The absolute numbers have fallen along with the proportions. Since 1972, the number of seniors scoring above 600 on the verbal exam is down 30 percent. Since 1981, the number of seniors scoring above 750 on both the verbal and math parts is down 50 percent.[20]

They sum up by writing that the broadening of post-secondary education led to a deterioration of the college track in American high schools. Textbooks (including vocabulary) were simplified. Grades were inflated. Less rigorous elective courses were allowed. Term papers became rare, and multiple-choice tests dominated. "By the early 1970s, high school seniors had spent all of their high school years in a weakened academic environment."[21] All of that hurts the superior students more than those with less academic potential. That seemed to be confirmed by a Department of Education study, *The Washington Post* report on which carried the unstartling headline: "Gifted Pupils Bored, Study Says; U.S. Finds Brightest Students Are Not Challenged."[22]

Even though Murray and Herrnstein argue in their article that for the entire school population, the quality of education has not dropped, they hasten to add that that does not exonerate the schools. "When the average American high school senior can score only about 375 on the SAT-verbal and 415 on the SAT-math, it makes little difference that he is doing about as well as his predecessors ever did. It is not good enough, especially if gainful employment increasingly depends on these academic skills, as it evidently does."[23]

Other tests show a fall in children's ability to reason. In 1990, the Educational Testing Service, summing up twenty years of data from the National Assessment of Educational Progress (NAEP) noted, "The NAEP results indicate a remarkable consistency across subject areas—students are learning facts and skills, but few show the capacity for complex reasoning and problem solving. . . . Most of the gains appear to have occurred in lower-level skills and basic concepts. . . . In contrast, most of the declines have occurred in the area of higher-level applications."[24]

Curiously, this slippage has occurred at the same time that "there is, in fact, considerable evidence to suggest that [IQ scores] are rising. . . . Today it is widely conceded that test scores are in a slow, long-term rise. . . . Overall, test scores have been increasing at a rate that seem to average about .3 IQ points per year, which translates into some 15 points during the past half century."[25] Many theories have been offered for the rise in IQ scores (see Seligman's excellent book), but the implications for the public schools are not good. Even in the face of an apparent increase in the general intelligence of America's children, the schools have gotten worse at preparing them for college.

Other pessimistic news came out of a nationwide study in 1986 of what 8,000 17-year-old students knew about history and literature. The federally funded study was conducted by the NAEP.[26] Overall, the students averaged 54.5 percent correct on the history part of the examination and 51.8 percent on the literature part, both failing grades.

Private school students scored better than public-school students in the study, but not much better. In history, Catholic school students scored an average 60 percent. Non-Catholic private-school students scored 63 percent. In literature, the scores were 58 and 60 percent, respectively. These weak scores perhaps show that not all of the problems are due to the public schools; they may be related to schooling per se. Nevertheless, the study found that private school students were more likely to be more knowledgeable than their public-school counterparts.[27]

The NAEP's 1992 assessment of fourth-, eighth-, and twelfth-graders showed the following results for 250,000 students in mathematics and 140,000 in reading:[28]

For math questions in which students had to give only a short answer, the average percentage correct was 42 for fourth grade, 53 for eighth, and 40 for twelfth. For math questions in which students had to explain the solutions to problems requiring a greater depth of understanding, the percentages correct were 16, 8, and 9, respectively.

In reading, the percentages of students meeting or exceeding the proficient level were 25, 28, and 37 for grades four, eight, and twelve, respectively. Private-school students had higher average reading proficiency than public school students.

Other measures of academic performance show the same dismal results. "Persuasive evidence shows that U.S. 13-year-olds lag far behind those of most other advanced nations" in math and science, writes education specialist Myron Lieberman. "The only exception is that U.S. 13-year-olds are slightly more proficient in science than 13-year-olds in Ireland."[29] He notes that the spread between the students of the U.S. and other nations is large. For example, while just 9 percent of U.S. 13-year-olds could deal with complex mathematics, 40 percent of Korean 13-year-olds could do so. The U.S. Department of Education wrote in 1991: "Among students in a group of advanced and developing countries, U.S. students had a mediocre performance on an international test of science proficiency. The U.S. students scored in the middle among the 10-year-olds, near the bottom among the 14-year-olds, and last among the 18-year-olds."[30]

Thomas Sowell points out that American students did worse on questions that required reasoning than on those that required knowledge of facts.[31]

Lieberman notes that literacy skills were also lacking in American students. He writes that only 48.4 percent of U.S. high school graduates could find information in a news article or an almanac, only 50.2 percent could follow travel directions on a map, and 49.4 percent could handle a checkbook register.[32]

Performance has not improved in the 1990s despite a decade of "reforms" prompted by the 1983 report, "A Nation at Risk," of the National Commission on Excellence in Education. That report, which lamented "a rising tide of mediocrity," spurred 42 states to toughen high-school graduation requirements and others to beef up teacher-certification programs. Forty percent of schools lengthened their school years, while others enacted other programs to encourage better student performance. Student-teacher ratios were reduced. Teacher salaries have increased 22 percent above the inflation rate since 1983, reaching a national average of $36,000. After all that, test scores have made no dramatic improvement.[33]

The international comparisons are more meaningful when we note that the United States spends more on primary and secondary education than virtually any other nation. In the mid 1980s, only Switzerland spent more per pupil than the United States. The touted Japanese education system spent only 54 percent of what the United States spent in 1985, according to the U.S. Department of Education.[34] "The cost of educating American students has been growing steadily and extravagantly," writes Lewis J. Perelman. "Since the 1950s U.S. real spending (constant dollars) for each K-12 pupil has quadrupled. . . . The United States today is spending over $40 billion more each year on K-12 education than it was at the beginning of the 1980s. Over the last decade, K-12 spending grew nearly 30% after adjusting for inflation."[35] Lieberman says the costs are understated.[36] For example, capital spending is not reflected in the per-student amounts.

There is no known correlation between spending and improvement in educational quality in the public schools. But that does not mean that money is irrelevant to providing a good education. Most of the increase has gone into bureaucracy. The public schools do not use money well, for reasons explained in Chapter 2.

There are certainly indications that students of years ago were more knowledgeable, at least in some ways, than today's students. For example, the *admissions* examination to Jersey City High School in 1885 included these questions:[37]

Algebra
1. Define a polynomial. Make a literal trinomial.
2. Write a homogeneous quadrinomial of the third degree.
    Express the cube root of $10ax$ in two ways.
Geography
Name four principal ranges of mountains in Asia, three in Europe, and three in Africa.

U.S. History
1. What event do you connect with 1565, 1607, 1620, 1664, 1775?
2. What caused the Mexican War? What was the result? What American general commanded at the capture of the City of Mexico?

Grammar
1. Write a sentence containing a noun used as an attribute, a verb in the perfect tense potential mood, and a proper adjective.
2. Write the declension of (a) bird, (b) man, (c) fly, (d) fox, (e) it.

How many college graduates could answer those questions today? (That high school students could pass that exam does not tell us whether the point of school is to end up with children who can handle those problems. But it does indicate how the schools have changed.)

Other measures

There are aspects to assessing the schools besides academic performance. Schools, particularly in the inner cities, are violent places and hardly institutions in which contemplative activities can take place. Some schools have to pass their students through metal detectors each morning to keep them from bringing guns to the classrooms. Children have been shot on school grounds, caught in the crossfire between young thugs. A 1993 survey by the National School Boards Association found that 82 percent (of 729 school districts responding) reported an increase in violence over the preceding five years. The survey showed that 39 percent of urban districts had a shooting or a stabbing in 1993; 23 percent had a drive-by shooting. Moreover, a Metropolitan Life study released in late 1993 reported that over 10 percent of teachers and about 25 percent of their students had been victims of violence in or near their public schools.[38]

This seems to be a problem exclusive to public schools. Why? Public schooling did not create violence (at least it was not alone in doing so), but it is not dealing with it very well, to say the least.

Apart from violence, a disturbing culture has arisen, especially in the inner cities, that denigrates learning and general accomplishments of the mind. That has discouraged children from fulfilling their potential and going on to live creative, productive lives. To the extent the public schools have been unable to prevent the rise of that anti-intellectual culture, and now to reverse it, it is guilty of one of the greatest crimes against children. That alone should make us wonder if there is a better way.

We cannot overlook the fact that after decades of allegedly value-free sex education and years of condom distribution, teenage pregnancy, with all the obvious problems it brings, shows no signs of abating. Pregnancies per thousand of unmarried women aged 15 to 19 rose from 12.6 in 1950 to 31.6 in 1985.[39] The issue is so commonplace that stories announcing another rise in the teenage pregnancy rate get buried in *The New York Times*. The schools are not fully to blame for that problem. The welfare system deserves the lion's share of the blame for subsidizing single-motherhood. But the public schools are part of the welfare state. And they are the institutions that promised parents and everyone else that it could play a constructive role in the formation of self-respect and other virtues.

Lieberman reminds us that virtually from the beginning, the advocates of public schools held themselves out as shapers of good character. The results are disheartening. "In fact," he writes, "crime rates have increased along with the proportion of children educated in public schools and the duration of their education."[40] Lieberman suggests that the higher crime can be explained by the fact that "free" education gives students no sense of investing in their own "human capital." "Individuals who have invested more of their own funds in building up their human capital are less likely to risk loss of their investment," he writes. "Investment in human capital by government is likely to be less effective than investment from personal funds in deterring crime."[41]

In recent years, the public schools have become battlegrounds in the culture wars raging in the nation. So-called liberals seek to impose "multiculturalism" on the curriculum while expunging anything deemed offensive to certain groups. They want young children taught about AIDS and homosexuality whether or not their parents think it is time. In New York and elsewhere, arrogant school officials have tried to impose offensive—in some parents' eyes even pornographic—curricula on first-graders, parents, and local school boards.[42] The religious right objected to much of this, but it has engaged in its own form of imposition at times by trying to have books removed from public school libraries and curricula rather than demanding choice. It has also pushed for school prayer and the teaching of creationism as science. As noted in Chapter 2, such problems are purely the creatures of public schools.

112

It is hard to escape the feeling that these problems do not plague the private and Catholic schools to the same extent they do the public schools.[43] Meanwhile, we note that parents see the private schools as a source of security for children. The suburban public schools fit somewhere between the urban schools and the private schools. But there is a sense that, at least in some places, they are in decline, as well.

What does it matter if the public schools are bad? The usual answer is that the United States cannot be competitive in the intensifying world economy if the schools are turning out uneducated students. As we will see, that national-collectivist answer is entirely consistent with the reason the public schools were created in the first place. But it is an unsatisfactory answer. The children do not exist for the sake of the nation; they should not be educated for its sake either. Education should make it possible for individuals to become the kind of people they wish to be. It should show them the virtue of thinking and learning. It should expose them to the things that are worthwhile knowing and thinking about. But it should not regard them as cogs in a great national economic machine. That is part of the reason the schools are in the mess they are in.

The backlash

Many advocates of public schools accept the evidence of decline and use it to lobby for more tax money. But some reject the claim that the schools are on the skids. One of the most tenacious defenders of the public schools' record is Gerald Bracey, a research psychologist and education consultant, who wrote in 1991 that "the overwhelming evidence shows that *American schools have never achieved more than they currently achieve*. And some indicators show them performing better than ever."[44] He pointed out that graduation rates are at record levels. He cited studies showing that while only 10 percent of 17-year-olds completed high school in 1910, by 1965 the proportion was 75 percent. "In 1989 about 83% of all students received a diploma 12 years after beginning school," he wrote.[45] The good old days, he added, were a time when the graduation rate was under 50 percent, and dropping out was without stigma or dire economic consequence. He does concede, however, that the gap between the best public schools and the worst has grown.

Of course, graduation rates may not be a sign of achievement if standards are lowered and if a sluggish economy makes it difficult for would-be dropouts to find jobs. Thus, what Bracey regards as achievement may, in fact, not be that at all.

Regarding the SAT, he notes that the composition of students taking the test is radically different from 1941 when the initial standards were set. In 1941, writes Bracey, the test takers were an elite group of somewhat more than 10,000 students—white, male, and northeastern. As the eighties closed, about a million students took the SAT, 27 percent members of minorities and 52 percent female. Thus, Bracey explains the decline in the average scores as a result of democratization of test taking. He writes that a group of test takers in 1990 with a profile similar to those in 1941 had average scores close to their 1941 counterparts—454 on the verbal test and 505 on the math test. Thus, he says, there has been no decline in the scores. He adds that the Preliminary Scholastic Aptitude Test, first administered in 1960, shows a similar consistency.

He contradicts Singal's point about the decline among top students. "The percentage of students scoring above 600 (above the 84th percentile) on the verbal subtest of the SAT fell until 1975 and then stabilized," Bracey writes. "The percentage of students scoring above 600 on the math subtest fell until 1975 and has recently returned to a level slightly above that of 1972."[46]

In his 1992 follow-up article, Bracey wrote that he puts little stock in achievement test scores because "I don't think they measure particularly important outcomes" and because they have diminished credibility. Even so, he argues that the data show test scores rising.[47] "When the results of national norming studies of the [Iowa Tests of Basic Skills] and [Iowa Tests of Educational Development] are placed on the Iowa trend lines, they fit well," meaning that scores fell in the late 1960s and early 1970s, then rose. The trend line in Iowa shows the ITBS scores rising to all-time highs for grades 3 through 7 in 1991, and nearly so in grade 8. The ITED scores were at all-time highs for grades 9, 10, and 11, and close to an all-time high for grade 12.[48]

Bracey also alleges that the Ravitch-Finn interpretation of a study of American 11th graders' knowledge of American history and literature (see above) was biased. Bracey writes that Dale Whittington concluded that Ravitch and Finn's "item selection techniques guaranteed low scores."[49] Moreover, Whittington finds no deterioration in students' knowledge after looking at studies done in 1917, 1933, 1944, and 1964. She sums up:

Comparisons of student performance on test questions that matched the content of specific questions used by Ravitch and Finn seem to confirm the results of this study that, for the most part, students of the 1980s are not demonstrably different from students of their parents' and grandparents' generation in terms of their knowledge of American history. . . . Indeed, given the reduced dropout rate and less elitist composition of the 17-year-old student body today, one could argue that students know more American history today than did their age peers of the past.[50]

Bracey writes that Whittington's results are typical of "then-and-now" studies of test scores.

Bracey similarly attacks international comparisons of student achievement, alleging severe methodological flaws and other problems. He suggests that although American students actually do as well or better in some areas as students in other countries, including the Japanese, problems such as poverty and broken families have consequences that are mistakenly blamed on the schools.[51]

But Bracey's writing is at war with itself. He complains that the public schools are blamed for things they are not responsible for. But if that is true, it is possible also to credit the schools with things they had nothing to do with. Just as we can imagine students doing worse on standardized tests even though the schools had not gotten worse, so can we imagine students doing better although the schools had not gotten better. People have the general impression that the schools worked better years ago. Maybe they did. But maybe they only seemed to work better because what actually worked better were families and communities. There is ample research showing that what matters for student performance is not the school per se or the per-pupil expenditure or the student-teacher ratio. It is the family. It is highly possible that the public schools in the "good old days" were getting credit that properly belongs to the family.

Problems in interpretation

In the battle between those who think the public schools work well and those who do not, each side has numerous studies to defend its position. The question is whether the matter can be resolved by tracking test scores and making international comparisons. Such studies are not worthless. The SAT is known as a good predictor of how students will do in school. It is also highly correlated with the IQ test, which itself is a good predictor of how people will do in their working lives.

But there is a danger of overinterpreting such studies. Pinpointing the cause of any social phenomenon, such as a fall in test scores, is tricky for the simple reason that there are always countless factors at work, and isolating any one is impossible. There is no social laboratory in which scientists in white coats, like physicists, can hold every variable but one constant.

As Ludwig von Mises wrote, "The experience with which the sciences of human action have to deal is always an experience of complex phenomena. No laboratory experiments can be performed with regard to human action. We are never in a position to observe the change in one element only, all other conditions of the event remaining unchanged."[52] The upshot is that when the critics and defenders of public schools finish trading numbers and studies, we are still faced with the task of logically sorting out what are the causes and what are the effects. Is a decline in SAT scores a sign of worsening schools? Is a stabilizing of scores a sign of improvement in the schools? Or are they signs of other things?

Similarly, are the signs of nonacademic deterioration in the public schools—arrests, pregnancy, drug use, etc.—versus the private schools symptomatic of government education? Or, as the public school defenders argue, do those schools begin with children more likely to commit crimes, get pregnant, and use drugs?

The numbers cannot tell us. Correlation is not causation. We must avoid the *post hoc ergo propter hoc* fallacy of assuming that if B follows A, then A caused B. Only theory can lead us out of the statistical thicket and create understanding.

Bracey makes some valid points. Is it a sign of deterioration that high school freshmen do not know algebra? Or is it a sign that we have learned that most people do not need to know algebra? Perhaps multi-hour exams that probe a student's inventory of disconnected facts are not a valid method of assessing his education. Perhaps if children do not do well by these standards, it does not reflect poorly on the schools. On the other hand, if a significant number of high school graduates don't know in what half-century the Civil War took place or that the words "from each according to his ability, to each according to his need" *do not* appear in the U.S. Constitution, that may say something about how the public schools are doing, especially since they promised to make good citizens out of our children. Moreover, how much do international comparisons tell us if other countries also have centralized, monopolized state-run systems? Even in a race of slow runners, someone has to finish first.

In the final analysis, to decide whether the public schools should be changed, left as they are, or abolished, one needs to understand *theoretically* what the public schools are and what the alternatives are. We have to analyze the detailed ramifications of government-produced schooling through the lens of sound theory concerning politics, economics, and ethics. That understanding, in turn, will enable us to form reasonable expectations about public schools and the alternatives. From there, each of us should be able to make an intelligent choice about how education should be achieved in American society.

Notes

[1] David Boaz, "The Public School Monopoly: America's Berlin Wall," in *Liberating Schools: Education in the Inner City*, ed. David Boaz (Washington, D.C.: Cato Institute), p. 9, Figure 1-2. The information comes from Denis P. Doyle and Terry W. Hartle, "Where Public School Teachers Send Their Children to School: A Preliminary Analysis" (Washington, D.C.: American Enterprise Institute, unpublished ms., n.d.)

[2] "This Week with David Brinkley," August 29, 1993. Albert Shanker, president of the American Federation of Teachers, says that is an exaggeration.

[3] Unpublished letter, dated September 29, 1993, to *Education Week*.

[4] "An Assessment of American Education: The View of Employers, Higher Educators, The Public, Recent Students, and Their Parents" (New York: Harris Education Research Center, Fall 1991), p. 6.

[5] Ibid. In September 1993, a Department of Education study found that nearly half of the nation's 191 million adults could not write a letter to explain a billing error or compute the length of a bus trip from a schedule. William Celis 3d, "Study Says Half of Adults in U.S. Can't Read or Handle Arithmetic," *The New York Times*, September 9, 1993, A1.

[6] "An Assessment of American Education."

[7] Ibid, p. 7. The survey showed only a "slightly more positive" score when educators were surveyed.

[8] Ibid., p. 10; emphasis in original.

[9] Jonathan Weisman, "Workforce Skills Hamper Productivity, Manufacturers Say," *Education Week*, December 11, 1991, p. 5.

[10] Ibid.

[11] Thomas Sowell, *Inside American Education: The Decline, The Deception, The Dogma* (New York: Free Press, 1993), p. 6. See also Daniel J. Singal, "The Other Crisis in Education," *The Atlantic Monthly*, November 1991.

[12] William A. Niskanen, "The Performance of America's Primary and Secondary Schools," in Boaz, pp. 57–58.

[13] Ibid., p. 59.

[14] Boaz, p. 2.

[15] Charles Murray and R. J. Herrnstein, "What's Really Behind the SAT-score Decline?" *Public Interest*, Winter 1992, p. 38.

[16] Ibid., p. 58.

[17] Ibid., pp. 34–35.

[18] Ibid., pp. 43–44.

[19] Ibid., pp. 48–49. See Singal, cited above.

[20] Pete du Pont, "Education Enterprise Zones," in Boaz, p. 207.

[21] Murray and Herrnstein, p. 52.

[22] November 5, 1993, p. A1.

[23] Murray and Herrnstein, pp. 53-54.

[24] Educational Testing Service, *America's Challenge: Accelerating Academic Achievement. A Summary of Findings from 20 Years of NAEP* (Princeton, N.J.: 1990), p. 33; quoted in Daniel Seligman, *A Question of Intelligence: The IQ Debate in America* (New York: Birch Lane Press, 1992), p. 170.

[25] Seligman, pp. 171–72.

[26] See Diane Ravitch and Chester E. Finn, Jr., *What Do Our 17-Year-Olds Know?* (New York: Harper & Row, 1987).

[27] Ibid., pp. 173–74.

[28] John A. Dossey et al., *Can Students Do Mathematical Problem Solving?* (Washington, D.C.: National Center for Education Statistics, U.S. Department of Education, Report No. 23-FR01, August 1993) and Ina V.S. Mullis et al., *NAEP 1992 Reading Report Card for the Nation and the States* (Washington, D.C.: National Center for Education Statistics, U.S. Department of Education, Report No. 23-ST06, September 1993).

[29] Myron Lieberman, *Public Education: An Autopsy* (Cambridge, Mass.: Harvard University Press, 1993), p. 145.

[30] Quoted in ibid., p. 145.

[31] Sowell, p. 4.

[32] Lieberman, p. 146.

[33] William Celis 3d, "10 Years After a Scathing Report, Schools Show Uneven Progress," *The New York Times*, April 28, 1993, p. A19. Also see Lawrence A. Uzzell, "Education Reform Fails the Test," *The Wall Street Journal*, May 10, 1989.

[34] Lewis J. Perelman, "The 'Acanemia' Deception," Hudson Institute Briefing Paper No. 120, May 1990, p. 3. Supporters of public

schools often lament that the United States spends a smaller portion of gross domestic product on education than other nations do. That is a misleading standard, since the United States has the largest per capita GDP in the world. What counts is absolute per-pupil spending.

[35] Ibid., p. 10.

[36] Lieberman, p. 126.

[37] *Men's Health*, June 1993, p. 53. Most people, of course, did not attend high school in 1885.

[38] "Survey of Schools Finds 'Epidemic of Violence,'" *The Washington Post* (Associated Press), January 6, 1994, A6, and Kenneth Eskey, "Schools Fight Losing Battle against Student Mayhem," *The Washington Times*, January 6, 1994, A6.

[39] Lieberman, p. 148.

[40] Ibid., p. 150. John R. Lott, Jr., has studied crime and the public schools and concludes that public education leads to higher crime. ("Juvenile Delinquency and Education: A Comparison of Public and Private Provision," *International Review of Law and Economics* 7 [1987], pp. 163–75; cited in Lieberman, p. 150.)

[41] Lieberman, p. 150.

[42] See William Tucker, "Revolt in Queens," *The American Spectator*, February 1993, pp. 26-31.

[43] James S. Coleman has argued the superiority of private schools in several books. See, for example, James S. Coleman and Thomas Hoffer, *Public and Private High Schools: The Impact of Communities* (New York: Basic Books, 1987). The argument that Catholic school students come from richer or better homes does not work. The results are similar for low-income students whose parents did not pay to send them to the schools. See Sowell, p. 10.

[44] Gerald Bracey, "Why Can't They Be Like We Were?" *Phi Delta Kappan*, October 1991, p. 106; emphasis in original.

[45] Ibid., p. 106. Of course, as Bracey points out, that percentage does not count students who get diplomas after their twelfth year in school.

[46] Ibid., p. 110.

[47] Gerald Bracey, "The Second Bracey Report on the Condition of Public Education," *Phi Delta Kappan*, October 1992, p. 107.

[48] Ibid., p. 107.

[49] Ibid., p. 107. Whittington's analysis appeared in "What Have Our 17-Year-Olds Known in the Past?" *American Educational Journal*, Winter 1992.

[50] Quoted in "Second Bracey Report," p. 107.

[51] In his third report (*Phi Delta Kappan*, October 1993) Bracey offers more of what he regards as evidence that the schools, except for those in the inner cities, work. See also *The New York Times*, December 9, 1993, A1, for the results of a comparison of schools involving European nations.

[52] Ludwig von Mises, *Human Action*, 3d revised edition (Chicago: Henry Regnery Company, 1966), p. 31.

About the Author

Sheldon Richman is senior editor at the Cato Institute, book review editor of the *Cato Journal*, contributing editor to *Regulation* magazine, and associate producer of "Cato Forum," a weekly cable/satellite television program.

Mr. Richman's articles on education and many other issues have appeared in *The Washington Post, The Wall Street Journal, The American Scholar, Chicago Tribune, USA Today, The Washington Times, Insight, Cato Policy Report, Journal of Economic Development, The Freeman, Reason, Washington Report on Middle East Affairs, Middle East Policy,* and *Liberty*. He is a contributor to *The Fortune Encyclopedia of Economics*.

A former newspaper reporter, associate editor of *Inquiry* magazine, and senior editor at the Institute for Humane Studies at George Mason University, Mr. Richman is a graduate of Temple University in Philadelphia.

About the Publisher

Founded in 1989, The Future of Freedom Foundation is a 501(c)(3), tax-exempt, educational foundation that presents an uncompromising moral, philosophical, and economic case for individual freedom, private property, and limited government.

The officers of The Foundation are: Jacob G. Hornberger (Fairfax, Virginia), president, and Richard M. Ebeling (Hillsdale, Michigan), vice president of academic affairs. There are nine members on the Foundation's board of trustees. *Freedom Daily* is published monthly by The Foundation. It consists of essays, book reviews, and quotes by freedom's greatest champions. Subscribers come from thirty countries. The price of a one-year subscription is $15 ($20 foreign). The Foundation also shares its ideas on liberty with others through lectures, speeches, seminars, and radio appearances.

The Foundation neither solicits nor accepts governmental funds. Operations are financed through subscription revenues and donations, which are invited in any amount. Please write us for additional information. We hope you join us in this important work!

The Future of Freedom Foundation
11350 Random Hills Road, Suite 800
Fairfax, Virginia 22030
(703) 934-6101
Fax (703) 803-1480

Index

L

Lazerson, Marvin, 43
Learning
  bias against abstract, 50
  in everyday life, 95
  family-based, 94-95
  homeschooler perception of, 92
  imposed in public school, xi-xii, 92
  opposition to forced (Spencer), 94
Libertarian philosophy, 6-7, 74, 70-71, 100-101
Liberty
  American belief in, xi
  public school antagonism, 51
  suppression by public school system, 70-71
  Voluntaryist position, 67-68
  See also Freedom
Lieberman, Myron, 13-14, 109-10, 112
Lippmann, Walter, 27-28
Literacy, 3, 38, 105
Lott, John R., Jr., 27
Luther, Martin, 40, 41

M

McReynolds, Justice James C., 85
Malthus, Thomas, 3
Mandela, Winnie, 51
Mann, Horace, 47-49
Mencken, H. L., 1, 70-71
Metropolitan Life Insurance Company study, 111
Mill, John Stuart, 26, 61
Mitchell, Richard, 28, 74, 84, 93
Moe, Terry M., 15-16, 20
Moral education
  common school provision of, 49
  government interference with, 23
Murphey, Archibald D., 46
Murray, Charles, 32, 64, 106-8

N

National Assessment of Educational Progress (NAEP), 108
National Association of Manufacturers study, 105
National Commission on Excellence in Education, 110
National Education Association, 92, 101
Nationalism
  of Noah Webster, 46-47
  public education teaching of, 71
National School Boards Association survey, 111
New Puritanism, 25
Niskanen, William A., 106
Nock, Albert Jay, 71

O

Owen, Robert Dale, 46

P

Parents
  ability to judge quality of education, 61-62
  circumstances for conflict with schools, 28-29
  as guardians and educators, xix, 20-21
  responsibility develops self-restraint, 63-64
  responsibility for child's education, 59
  right to educate children, 87
  as viewed by public school system, xiv-xv, 20-26, 51-52
Paterson, Isabel, 71-73
Peltzman, Sam, 17
Perelman, Lewis J., 90, 110
Pierce v. Society of Sisters, 85
Poulson, Barry, 47
Priestly, Joseph, 57, 69
Privatization, 88-89
Procter and Gamble survey, 24
Progressive education movement
  critics of, 71-72
  principles of, 50
Propaganda, xviii-xix, 10, 39-40, 68, 73
Property tax, 11-12, 17, 30
Public goods theory, 19-20
Public school movement, 57

R

Rand, Ayn, 74
Read, Leonard, 74
Reform
  charter school movement, 82
  contracting out, 82-83
  voucher plan, 83-85
Ritalin, 25, 82
Roberts, Stephen H., xvii
Ross, Edward, 49-50
Rothbard, Murray N., 29, 31, 74
Rush, Benjamin, 37, 45
Rust, Bernhard, xvii

S

Scholastic Aptitude Test (SAT)
  composition of students taking, 113-14
  scores, 106-7
School choice
  definition of free, 75
  private schools, 22
  public schools, 22
Schools
  as agencies of society, 20
  as community enterprise, 4
  as jails, 86